WORLD DOMINATION

The Operator's Manual

What Wall Street, Hedge Funds & the Government Don't Want You to Know

ALSO BY THE AUTHOR

The Operator Edition Trilogy

Book One

THE OPERATOR'S BLUEPRINT

The Mindset, the Map, and the Mission

Book Two

THE OPERATOR'S PLAYBOOK

Execution, Tactics, and Building Wealth From the Ground Up

WORLD DOMINATION

The Operator's Manual

What Wall Street, Hedge Funds, and the Government Don't Want You to Know

OPERATOR EDITION - BOOK THREE

Disclaimer: This book is for educational and informational purposes only. Nothing in this book constitutes financial, legal, investment, or tax advice. The author is not a licensed financial advisor, attorney, or tax professional. All strategies discussed are general in nature. Consult a qualified professional before making any financial decisions. Results vary. Past performance is not indicative of future results.

Published in the United States of America

First Edition, 2026

DEDICATION

To my family - the ones who accepted me back when I didn't deserve it. To my anonymous family - without you, I would not still be here. "Dreams come true... they just haven't happened yet." R.I.P. Esther, for telling me that when I needed it most.

To my daughter, Cheyanne - your love moves mountains. You gave my life new meaning.

And to the readers - understand this clearly: you are not fans, and you are not followers. I don't do followers. You're Operators. You're here because you want to change your world, not watch someone else change theirs. If this book helps you do that, then every word was worth writing.

"The most dangerous person in any room is not the one who makes the most noise. It is the one who has quietly learned how everything in the room was built, and by whom, and why and is already three moves ahead."

-The Operator's Creed

FOREWORD

I didn't plan to write three books.

When I started this series, I had one goal: give people the framework they were never handed. Not the sanitized, compliance-approved version of personal finance that most books deliver - the kind that talks about index funds and lattes and compound interest in ways that make you feel vaguely guilty about your spending habits but leave you no closer to understanding how actual wealth is built. I wanted to write something that felt like sitting across the table from someone who had been inside the machine, who knew where the levers were, and who had decided to stop pretending those levers were a secret.

Book 1, *The Operator's Blueprint*, was about rewiring the way you think. Before any strategy matters, before any tactic lands, you have to fix the operating system. Most people who fail financially don't fail because they lack information. They fail because they carry beliefs about money that were installed before they were old enough to question them - beliefs that serve the financial system's interests, not theirs.

Book 1 was the deconstruction of those beliefs and the installation of an Operator's mindset: ownership, intentionality, and ruthless financial self-awareness.

Book 2, *The Operator's Playbook*, was where we got tactical. Real estate. Business structure. Market mechanics. How to build multiple income streams from where you are, with what you have, in the actual world rather than in a finance textbook's imaginary frictionless economy. People who came through Book 2 changed the way they spent, saved, invested, and built not with some radical transformation, but with the quiet confidence that comes from finally knowing what you're doing.

But something kept nagging at me. Every question I received, every conversation at an event or in a message, kept circling back to a deeper layer. People who had read the first two books were executing, they were doing the work and yet they kept running into walls they couldn't explain. Deals that didn't close for reasons that had nothing to do with the deal. Markets that moved in ways that felt orchestrated. Tax bills that seemed disconnected from anything they understood about how taxes worked. Regulations that appeared designed to protect someone, but not them. A sense that even when they were playing correctly, the scoreboard was tilted.

That nagging feeling is what this book is about.

The financial establishment and I use that term deliberately, as an institution with shared interests rather than a conspiracy of mustache-twirling villains has a vested interest in keeping the architecture of power opaque. Not because there's a meeting room somewhere where people actively decide to deceive ordinary citizens, but because opacity is simply more profitable. When the rules of the game are unclear, the people who know the rules win. And the people who wrote the rules make sure they know them better than anyone.

This book is about peeling back that opacity. Chapter by chapter, we will walk through how the financial system was actually constructed, who benefits from that construction, and how an Operator navigates it intelligently. Not by rejecting the system the system isn't going anywhere, and pretending you can opt out of it entirely is a fantasy that tends to end in either poverty or prison. But by understanding the system at a level that most people never reach, an Operator can move through it with a precision that looks, from the outside, like magic.

This is Book 3. It is the master-level playbook. It assumes you've done the internal work. It assumes you've begun building. Now it's time to learn the whole board the global systems, the power structures, the tools that institutions use but rarely discuss publicly, and the philosophy that holds it all together.

Some of what you read here will anger you. Good. Anger, properly directed, is fuel. Some of it will surprise you. Good. Surprise means you're learning. Some of it will clarify things that have confused you for years and that clarity is what we're after.

Welcome to the final level.

The operation doesn't end when you close this book. But by the time you get there, you'll know exactly what to do next.

The Author
2026

TABLE OF CONTENTS

Introduction

The Game behind the Game

There is a game most people play. You probably know it well. Work hard, save money, contribute to your 401(k), buy a house in a good neighborhood, diversify your portfolio, don't take on too much debt, and eventually, after forty years of disciplined effort, you'll have enough to retire comfortably. Maybe, if nothing goes catastrophically wrong, if you don't get sick, if the market cooperates, if inflation doesn't devour what you've built.

This is the game the financial establishment designed for ordinary people. Not maliciously. Not necessarily with any grand intention to harm. But with a clear structural purpose: to keep capital moving through the institutions that profit from managing it, investing it, lending it out, insuring it, and taxing it. The game was designed to make you a participant, a necessary participant, someone whose contributions fund the whole operation without ever quite making you a principal. A participant plays the game. A principal owns a piece of it.

Most financial education is participant education. It teaches you how to be a better player in a game you didn't design, with rules you didn't write, on a field that tilts in ways you've been taught not to notice. And in fairness, playing the participant game competently is infinitely better than not playing at all. The person who maxes out their 401(k) for thirty years and buys index funds and avoids catastrophic debt will end up in far better shape than the person who does none of those things. Participant-level financial literacy matters.

But it's not enough. Not for what we're building.

This book is about the game behind the game, the deeper layer of financial reality that governs how wealth is actually created, concentrated, protected, and transferred across generations. It's the layer where the principals operate. Where the rules are still rules, but the players who know them have access to legal structures, tax strategies, global tools, and institutional knowledge that the participant game never mentions.

What "World Domination" Means to an Operator

The title of this book is deliberately provocative. World domination. It sounds like a villain's monologue. It's not.

In Operator terms, world domination means exactly this: complete command of your financial universe. Not dominance over other people. Not the accumulation of wealth at the expense of others. Not the hoarding of resources or the exploitation of the vulnerable. Those are what happens when people who acquire power do so without wisdom, integrity, or purpose, and their stories tend to end badly, as we'll see in Part Three.

Operator-level world domination is about sovereignty. It means you are no longer waiting for someone else's system to determine your financial destiny. You understand the forces at work in the global economy. You have positioned yourself, your assets, your income streams, your entity structures, your tax strategy to operate with intentionality at every level. You are not a passenger. You are not a product. You are an Operator, and you command your operation with full situational awareness and strategic precision.

That is the ambition of this book. Not fantasy - strategy. Not rebellion - mastery.

What You Will Learn

We begin in Part One by pulling back the curtain on the architecture of the financial system itself. Most people have a vague understanding that "the system" exists and that it seems to benefit some people more than others. Part One makes that explicit, concrete, and useful. You will understand how central banking actually works, what investment banks are really doing when they trade on your behalf, how the government's relationship with capital has been structured over decades, and what central banks do that moves global markets in ways the evening news never quite explains.

Part Two is the global toolkit; the legal, strategic, and tactical instruments that sophisticated Operators actually use. International markets and currency dynamics. Offshore structures (legal, ethical, and explained without the mythology that surrounds them). Tax strategy at a level that goes far beyond "put money in a Roth IRA." Alternative assets that institutions have used for decades but that individual investors are only recently beginning to access.

And leverage - perhaps the most misunderstood and misused tool in the financial world - examined with the honesty it deserves.

Part Three studies the Operators who changed the game - those who built extraordinary wealth outside conventional wisdom, those who catastrophically failed and what their failures teach us, and how the digital revolution has fundamentally reshuffled the information landscape in ways that create genuine opportunity for the prepared.

Part Four is construction. You will build your personal financial command center: the entity structure, the banking stack, the income architecture, the legal and financial armor that protects everything you're building. And you will learn to think beyond your own lifetime because generational wealth is not an accident. It is an engineered outcome.

Part Five is philosophy. Because at the highest level, financial domination is not a technical problem, it is a psychological and ethical one. The most dangerous thing that can happen to an Operator is to acquire power without wisdom. Part Five is about making sure that doesn't happen to you.

A Word on How to Use This Book

This is not a book you read once and shelve. It is a reference, a manual, and if you engage with it seriously, a transformation. Read it straight through the first time, because the narrative builds. Then return to the chapters most relevant to your current phase of the operation. The chapter on tax strategy will mean something very different to you in five years than it does today. The chapter on generational wealth will hit differently once you have something worth protecting.

You have done the mindset work. You have done the execution work. Now it is time to understand the whole board.

Let's begin.

PART ONE:

How the system really Works

Chapter 1

The Architecture of Wealth: Who Built This Game and Why

"Give me control of a nation's money and I care not who makes its laws." attributed to Mayer Amschel Rothschild

Every game has rules. Every set of rules has an author. And in every game where real stakes are involved, the author of the rules has a reason for writing them the way they did. The global financial system is no different, it's just that almost no one ever asks who wrote the rules, when they wrote them, and whose interests they were protecting at the time.

This is where we start. Not with theory, not with abstract economics, but with the concrete historical reality of how the architecture of wealth was constructed. Because once you understand who built this system and why, every single aspect of how money moves in the modern world makes a new kind of sense. Not a comforting sense. But a useful one.

The Long History of Concentrated Power

Wealth concentration is not a modern phenomenon. It is as old as civilization itself. Every major society in human history has developed systems that tend, over time, to move wealth toward those who already have it. This is not a moral observation; it is a structural one. Wealth produces returns. Returns compound. Compounded returns, over time, concentrate into fewer and fewer hands unless some external force intervenes.

In ancient agricultural societies, that external force was often conquest. A neighboring civilization showed up, redistributed the land, and the cycle started over. In medieval Europe, it was the occasional plague that wiped out enough of the population to dramatically increase the bargaining power of the surviving peasantry, not exactly an efficient wealth redistribution mechanism, but historically effective. In the modern world, the external forces are taxes, regulation, and the occasional market crash, which not coincidentally tend to hurt the less wealthy more than the extremely wealthy, because the extremely wealthy own assets that recover while the less wealthy own labor that loses value.

What changed in the last three or four centuries and this is crucial to understand, is that wealth concentration stopped being primarily about land, military power, or royal favor. It became about the control of money itself. Specifically, the control of the supply and distribution of money. And the mechanism through which that control was achieved and institutionalized is the modern banking system.

To understand the modern financial architecture, you have to go back to the goldsmiths of seventeenth-century England. These were craftsmen who had the most secure storage facilities in town, they worked with gold, so they needed vaults and people began depositing their gold with them for safekeeping. In return, the goldsmiths issued receipts: pieces of paper that said "this receipt is good for X amount of gold." People began trading the receipts instead of moving the gold around. The receipts became, effectively, money.

Here's where the crucial insight emerged. The goldsmiths noticed something. At any given time, only a small fraction of their depositors came to claim their gold simultaneously. Most depositors left their gold sitting in the vault and just used the receipts. So the goldsmiths began issuing *more receipts than they had gold,* lending out receipts to borrowers and charging interest, knowing that as long as everyone didn't come for their gold at once, the scheme would hold. This is the origin of fractional reserve banking. It is, depending on your perspective, either a brilliant financial innovation that enables economic growth or the foundational fraud upon which the entire modern monetary system is built. It is probably both.

The goldsmiths became the first bankers. The receipts became the first paper currency. The practice of lending out more money than you have in reserve became institutionalized, legalized, and regulated not eliminated, but managed. And the people who controlled this system of money creation accumulated extraordinary power, because controlling money means controlling what gets built, what gets funded, who gets the resources to pursue their ambitions and who doesn't.

Central Banking Decoded

The central bank is the apex of the modern financial architecture. In the United States, that institution is the Federal Reserve, established in 1913. In Europe, it's the European Central Bank. In Britain, the Bank of England, which dates to 1694 and is one of the oldest central banks in the world? These institutions sit at the top of the monetary pyramid, and their decisions affect the price of every asset, the cost of every loan, the value of every dollar in your pocket, and the trajectory of every investment you will ever make.

Here is what most people understand about central banks: they control interest rates. They print money. They do something with inflation. Beyond that, the average person's understanding gets hazy, which is exactly the level of public understanding central banks tend to prefer.

Here is what an Operator understands about central banks:

First, central banks are not government agencies in the way most people assume. The Federal Reserve, for example, is a public-private hybrid. It was created by Congress and its chairman is appointed by the President, but its regional Federal Reserve Banks are owned by private member banks, the same commercial banks whose behavior the Fed is supposed to regulate. This creates a structural conflict of interest that has been debated since the Fed's founding, and that debate hasn't gotten any less relevant.

Second, the primary mechanism through which central banks influence the economy is the manipulation of the cost of money, interest rates. When the Fed raises rates, borrowing becomes more expensive, economic activity tends to slow, inflation tends to come down, and assets that are priced on the basis of future earnings tend to fall in value because those future earnings are discounted at a higher rate. When the Fed cuts rates, borrowing becomes cheaper, economic activity accelerates, inflation tends to rise, and assets particularly financial assets and real estate tend to appreciate. This is the basic mechanism. An Operator internalizes it and watches it constantly, because interest rate cycles are the single most predictable macro force in the financial world.

Third, and this is the piece that most people miss entirely: central banks have, over the past two decades, significantly expanded their toolkit beyond interest rate manipulation. Quantitative easing the practice of creating new money to purchase assets, primarily government bonds and, in the case of the Fed, mortgage-backed securities have become a standard tool. When the Fed conducts quantitative easing, it purchases these assets from financial institutions, injecting money into the financial system. That money tends to flow into financial assets, which is one major reason why financial assets have consistently outperformed wages and consumer prices since the 2008 financial crisis. If you owned assets, quantitative easing made you richer. If you owned primarily your own labor, it made you relatively poorer. This is not a conspiracy. It is a structural consequence of monetary policy that benefited asset owners at the expense of non-asset owners and understanding it explains a great deal about the wealth gap that has widened over the past fifteen years.

Fractional Reserve: The Magic Trick Explained

Let's be very concrete about fractional reserve banking because this is the mechanism most people never fully grasp, and grasping it changes the way you see every financial institution you will ever deal with.

You deposit $10,000 in a bank. You think the bank holds that $10,000 for you, ready to be returned on demand. The bank does hold a fraction of it, let's say 10%, or $1,000, as reserves (either in its vault or on deposit at the Federal Reserve). The remaining $9,000 it lends out to a borrower.

That borrower deposits their $9,000 in a bank (possibly the same one). The bank holds 10% of $900 and lends out $8,100. That $8,100 gets deposited. The bank holds $810 and lends out $7,290. And on and on, through a chain of loans and deposits, until your original $10,000 has effectively become nearly $100,000 in circulating money.

Your $10,000 deposit did not just sit in a vault. It became the seed of $100,000 in money supply. The bank did not have the $100,000 before you walked in the act of banking itself created it. This is called the money multiplier effect, and it is the foundation of how money is created in the modern economy. Not by printing presses, primarily by lending.

The implications of this for an Operator are significant. Banks are not neutral custodians of money. They are money-creation machines whose business model depends on perpetual growth in lending. This means they have a structural incentive to lend as much as possible to creditworthy borrowers. It also means that when the lending cycle reverses, when loans go bad and banks contract credit the effect on the economy is not just a reduction in money availability; it is a contraction in the money supply itself, which amplifies the downturn. This is what happened in 2008. It is what central banks are always trying to prevent from happening again. And it is why understanding the credit cycle, the expansion and contraction of lending across the economy is one of the most important macroeconomic frameworks an Operator can possess.

The Rules Were Written by the Winners

Here is the part that tends to make people uncomfortable, and then, once they've sat with it, tends to make them extremely focused.

The rules of the financial game - the tax code, the regulatory framework, the structure of financial institutions, the legal definitions of what counts as an investment versus speculation versus income were not written by neutral technocrats in the public interest. They were written by legislators, and legislators were advised by lobbyists, and lobbyists represent clients, and clients are the institutions and individuals who already have significant wealth and a direct financial interest in the shape of the rules.

This is not a shocking revelation. It is simply what happens in any system where rules are made by people who can be influenced and where influence is purchased with resources. The people with the most resources buy the most influence. The rules end up reflecting their interests. And then the rules, once established, make it easier for those people to accumulate more resources, which they use to purchase more influence. It is a self-reinforcing cycle, and it has been running for a very long time.

Specifically, look at the tax code. The distinction between "ordinary income" (taxed at rates up to 37% for high earners as of the time of this writing) and "capital gains" (taxed at up to 20% for long-term gains) did not emerge from any neutral analysis of optimal tax policy. It emerged from decades of lobbying by investment industry participants who earn primarily capital gains and have a direct financial interest in that category of income being taxed at lower rates than wages. The carried interest provision, which allows hedge fund and private equity managers to treat a substantial portion of their compensation as capital gains rather than ordinary income, has survived every political attempt to eliminate it for the same reason: the people it benefits are very good at making donations and very good at making arguments to legislators about why it should remain.

Now. Here is the Operator's response to all of this: not outrage, not cynicism, and certainly not paralysis. The response is: *learn the rules.*

Because here is what the rules also do: they create opportunities. The same tax code that seems to favor the wealthy also contains provisions legal, legitimate, and available to anyone who qualifies that allow ordinary people to significantly reduce their tax burden if they structure their financial lives correctly. The same regulatory framework that protects large institutions also creates spaces for smaller operators to maneuver. The same financial system that concentrates wealth also creates pathways in real estate, in business, in markets - for those who understand how it works to accelerate their own wealth-building dramatically.

The Operator does not play the victim in this story. The Operator studies the architecture of the system with cold precision, identifies the rules that can be used to their advantage, and builds accordingly. That is what the rest of this book is about.

Operator Insight: The Architecture Principle

Before you can win any game, you must understand who designed the game and what they were optimizing for. The financial system was designed to serve the interests of capital. If you control capital, the system serves you. The path to controlling capital begins with understanding how it moves, where it concentrates, and what rules govern its flow. Every chapter in this book adds a layer to that understanding.

What Operators know that civilians don't is simply this: the system is not a mystery. It is a machine. Machines can be studied. Machines can be understood. And once understood they can be operated. The question is not whether the machine is fair - it isn't, entirely but whether you are willing to learn how it works well enough to make it work for you.

In the chapters that follow, we are going to take the machine apart piece by piece, Wall Street. Government. Central banks, Global capital flows. By the time we're done with Part One, you will see the financial world through different eyes not cynical eyes, but clear ones. And clarity, in this game, is the most powerful asset you can have.

Chapter 2

Wall Street's Real Business Model

"Wall Street never changes, the pockets change, the suckers change, but Wall Street never changes, because human nature never changes." **Jesse Livermore**

Here is the most important thing you need to understand about Wall Street: it does not exist to make you rich. It exists to make money. Those two things occasionally overlap, and when they do, Wall Street will serve you admirably. But the moment your financial interests diverge from Wall Street's financial interests and they diverge far more often than the industry's marketing materials suggest - you will lose, consistently and predictably, unless you understand the game being played.

Wall Street is not a monolith. It is an ecosystem of competing institutions, each with its own business model, its own incentive structure, and its own relationship to the retail investor's money. Investment banks. Retail brokerages. Market makers. Prime brokers. Hedge funds. Asset managers. They all play different roles in the same drama. The Operator understands each role, because understanding the roles tells you where the conflicts of interest are and where there are conflicts of interest, there are places where you need to be particularly careful.

What Investment Banks Actually Do

Let's start with investment banks, because they are the gravitational center of Wall Street and because most people have only the vaguest idea of what they actually do.

Investment banks do several things. They underwrite securities meaning when a company wants to raise capital by selling stock or bonds to the public, the investment bank manages that process. It helps set the price, buys the securities from the issuer, and then sells them to investors. The bank profits from the spread between what it pays the issuer and what it sells the securities for to investors. This is the banking business in its most traditional form.

But that's only the beginning. Investment banks also trade securities for their own accounts what's called proprietary trading, or "prop trading." After the 2008 financial crisis, the Volcker Rule (part of the Dodd-Frank Act) restricted this activity for banks that also accept deposits, but the restriction is more porous than its proponents hoped. Investment banks also run asset management divisions that manage money for institutional clients. They run prime brokerage operations that provide services; financing, securities lending, research to hedge funds. They advise on mergers and acquisitions. They structure complex financial products, derivatives, collateralized debt obligations, structured notes and sell them to whoever will buy them.

The key thing to understand about all of these activities is this: the investment bank's primary fiduciary obligation is to itself. Not to you. Not to the issuer. To itself. This is not a scandal; it is a legal structure. Investment banks operate as principals, not agents, in most of their transactions. When Goldman Sachs sells you a structured product, it is not acting as your advisor. It is acting as a counterparty. And counterparties optimize for their own position, not yours.

The famous example of this dynamic played out spectacularly in the lead-up to the 2008 financial crisis, when multiple investment banks packaged mortgage-backed securities they knew to be of questionable quality, sold them to institutional clients, and in some cases simultaneously shorted the same securities betting that they would fall in value. Whether this rose to the level of fraud was the subject of years of litigation. What is beyond dispute is that it illustrated, in neon terms, the fundamental principle: Wall Street's business model is to make money. Yours is to make money too. These objectives will not always align.

The Retail Investor as Product

Now let's talk about you - the retail investor. And let's be blunt about your role in the Wall Street ecosystem.

You are not primarily a customer. You are primarily a source of revenue and in some important structural ways, you are the product.

This is not a metaphor. It is an economic reality that was made explicit when the practice of payment for order flow became widely understood following the GameStop saga of 2021. But to understand payment for order flow, you need to understand market structure first.

When you place a trade through a brokerage; let's say you want to buy 100 shares of Apple stock, your order needs to be executed somewhere. There are multiple venues where it can be executed: the major exchanges like the NYSE and

NASDAQ, and off-exchange venues operated by market makers. Your brokerage has a choice of where to send your order. In theory, it should send your order to wherever you'll get the best price. In practice, it often sends your order to the venue that pays it the most for the privilege of executing your trade. That payment is called payment for order flow, or PFOF.

The firm receiving your order typically a high-frequency trading firm or market maker like Citadel Securities or Virtu Financial makes money on the spread between the bid and ask price of the stock. Because they're receiving a large volume of retail orders, they can statistically predict the direction of retail flow and position themselves accordingly. They profit. The brokerage gets paid for sending them your order. You get "free" trading. Everybody wins except that you might have gotten a slightly better execution price if your order had gone somewhere else, and the aggregate cost of those slightly worse executions across millions of trades is not zero.

The "commission-free trading" revolution didn't eliminate the cost of trading. It changed who paid and how. Before commission-free trading, you paid a commission. Now, the payment comes from the information value of your order flow. You are still paying. You are just paying with the value of information about your behavior rather than with a direct fee.

This is not inherently evil. It is a business model. But an Operator should understand it clearly, because understanding it explains several things: why brokerage apps are designed to encourage frequent trading (each trade generates order flow to sell), why certain brokerages are very interested in keeping you engaged with their platform, and why "free" is never actually free in financial services.

Dark Pools, Payment for Order Flow, and Front-Running

Beyond payment for order flow, there are darker corners of market structure that deserve the Operator's attention.

Dark pools are private exchanges, trading venues operated by investment banks and other institutions where large blocks of stock can be traded without being visible to the public market. The purpose, from the institution's perspective, is legitimate: if you're a pension fund trying to sell five million shares of a company, you don't want your intention to sell visible to the entire market, because the moment the market knows a five-million-share sell order is coming, the price will drop before you can execute. Dark pools allow large institutional orders to be matched confidentially.

The problem with dark pools is that they fragment price discovery. When significant trading activity happens outside the public market, the "price" that everyone sees on the exchange is based on incomplete information about supply and demand. This benefits large institutions who have access to dark pools and disadvantages retail investors, who are trading against a price signal that doesn't reflect all available information.

Front-running is a related concept, though the legal definition matters here. Illegal front-running occurs when a broker or trader receives advance knowledge of a large client order, knowledge they have a duty not to exploit and trades for their own account ahead of that order to profit from the price movement the order will cause. This is unambiguously illegal and does happen, though prosecutions are relatively rare because proving intent is difficult.

Legal "front-running" sometimes called latency arbitrage occurs when high-frequency trading firms use faster data connections and co-location at exchanges (meaning their servers are physically located next to the exchange's servers) to receive market data and respond to it milliseconds before slower participants can. This is legal. It is also a direct information advantage that the HFT firm has over you. When you see a stock quoted at $50.00 bid and $50.02 ask and you place a market order to buy, the HFT firm may have already moved the price slightly against you by the time your order arrives. The difference is fractions of a cent on each share trivial on any individual trade, significant in aggregate across millions of retail trades per day.

The Operator's response to all of this is not to rage against the machine, but to operate with awareness. Use limit orders instead of market orders, particularly for less liquid securities, so you control the price at which you execute rather than accepting whatever the market gives you. Be thoughtful about the brokerage you use and understand their execution quality, not just their commission structure. For very large trades, consider whether institutional-grade execution (available through some platforms) makes economic sense.

Hedge Funds: Reality vs. Mythology

Few financial institutions carry as much mythology as hedge funds. They occupy a specific place in the cultural imagination secretive, brilliant, ruthless, generating impossible returns through strategies that ordinary mortals can't access or understand. The reality is more interesting and more complicated than the mythology.

A hedge fund is, at its most basic level, a pooled investment vehicle with relatively few regulatory constraints compared to a mutual fund. While mutual funds are heavily regulated under the Investment Company Act of 1940, they must maintain diversification, must value assets daily, must allow investors to redeem shares daily; hedge funds are structured to exempt themselves from these requirements by limiting their investors to "accredited investors" (those with a high income or net worth) and "qualified purchasers" (an even more restrictive category). This regulatory freedom allows hedge funds to do things mutual funds cannot: short stocks, use significant leverage, hold illiquid investments, pursue complex derivative strategies, and charge performance fees.

The standard hedge fund fee structure historically called "2 and 20" charges investors 2% of assets under management per year and 20% of profits above a certain threshold (the "high water mark"). This fee structure is extraordinary when you think about it carefully. Consider: a hedge fund managing $1 billion charges $20 million per year just to exist, before generating a single dollar of return for investors. And then takes 20% of whatever profits it generates above the previous peak. The incentive this creates is for growth in assets under management because more AUM means more management fees and for swinging for the fences on individual bets, because the manager captures 20% of the upside but doesn't share proportionally in the downside (the worst outcome for the manager is that the fund closes; they don't write checks to investors when they lose).

This is not to say hedge funds are worthless. Some are genuinely excellent, they provide uncorrelated returns, sophisticated risk management, and access to strategies that can protect a portfolio in ways that conventional investments cannot. The point is to understand the incentive structure clearly. The hedge fund manager's incentives and your incentives as an investor are not perfectly aligned, and the ways in which they diverge should inform how you evaluate any fund you might consider.

The other important reality about hedge funds: most of them underperform simple index funds over long time periods after fees. The data on this is fairly robust. The average hedge fund has not beaten a simple S&P 500 index fund on a risk-adjusted, after-fee basis over most ten-year periods since the 1990s. The exceptions — the truly excellent funds with genuine, sustainable edges — exist but are difficult to identify in advance and typically not open to new investors by the time their track records are compelling.

In Parts Two and Eight, we will look at how Operators can replicate certain hedge fund strategies at a smaller scale without paying the 2-and-20 fee structure. But for now, the Operator principle is this: understand what you're paying for and make sure you're actually getting it.

OPERATOR INSIGHT: THE INCENTIVE ALIGNMENT TEST

Before entering any financial relationship with a broker, an advisor, a fund manager, a bank; ask yourself: How does this person make money? Where do their incentives align with mine, and where do they diverge? You are not looking for perfection. You are looking for clarity. An advisor who charges you a flat fee for advice has different incentives than one who earns commissions on what they sell you. Neither is automatically good or bad, but you should know which one you're dealing with.

Wall Street is a sophisticated ecosystem that has been optimized over decades for one purpose: extracting maximum value from the capital that flows through it while providing enough return to keep capital flowing. An Operator navigates this ecosystem not with fear or contempt, but with clear eyes and a thorough understanding of where the incentives run. The tools Wall Street provides markets, leverage, derivatives, access to capital are genuinely powerful. Using them intelligently requires knowing exactly how the system that surrounds them works.

Chapter 3

The Government's Role: Protector or Participant?

"The modern conservative is engaged in one of man's oldest exercises in moral philosophy; that is, the search for a superior moral justification for selfishness." **John Kenneth Galbraith**

The answer to the question in this chapter's title is: both. The government is simultaneously the protector of the financial system's stability and a participant in the system's benefits. This is not a cynical observation, it is an accurate description of how democratic governments with market economies actually function. The Operator understands this dual role without illusion, and more importantly, understands how to use it.

Most people think of government regulation in binary terms: either the government is protecting them from predatory capitalism, or the government is getting in the way of free enterprise. The reality is more nuanced and, for an Operator, more actionable. Government creates the framework within which the financial game is played. That framework includes rules that genuinely protect ordinary citizens, deposit insurance, securities disclosure requirements, consumer financial protection laws and rules that primarily serve large capital interests. The Operator's job is to know which is which.

The Revolving Door

There is a phenomenon in Washington that has been documented extensively, criticized across the political spectrum, and yet persists with remarkable durability: the revolving door between financial regulators and the institutions they regulate.

The pattern works like this. A person spends a career in government at the Securities and Exchange Commission, the Commodity Futures Trading Commission, the Treasury Department, the Federal Reserve building expertise in financial regulation. They develop relationships with industry players. They understand the rules in deep, granular detail. And then, at some point, they leave government for a position at a financial institution, a law firm, or a lobbying shop, where their knowledge, relationships, and regulatory access are enormously valuable. The institution pays them very well for this value. Sometimes the flow goes the other direction: a person with deep industry expertise moves into a regulatory role for a few years, then returns to the private sector.

The revolving door exists because financial regulation is genuinely complex, and the expertise required to regulate it effectively is rare. Government agencies struggle to compete with private sector salaries, so they often can't retain their best people. The institutions being regulated actively recruit from the regulatory agencies because the expertise is valuable. None of this requires any conspiratorial intent. It is the natural result of a system where regulatory expertise is rare and private sector compensation is high.

The consequence, though, is structural: regulators know that their career after government often runs through the institutions they currently regulate. This creates an unconscious incentive even among well-intentioned people to avoid regulatory actions that would make future employment difficult. It also means that the major financial institutions have a steady supply of former regulators who know exactly how the enforcement machinery works, where its limits are, and how to structure activities to stay on the right side of the line. Or very close to it.

The Operator's practical takeaway from this: regulations are not neutral. They are negotiated. The shape of any given regulation reflects the interests of the parties who participated most actively in its drafting, and large financial institutions participate very actively indeed. This means that regulations often contain provisions that benefit large institutions at the expense of smaller competitors, and provisions that create compliance costs substantial enough to winnow out smaller players who can't afford the legal and compliance infrastructure.

Policy as Wealth Protection

The 2008 financial crisis and its aftermath provide the clearest modern illustration of how government policy functions as a mechanism of wealth protection specifically, whose wealth gets protected.

When the housing market collapsed and major financial institutions faced insolvency, the government's response was a series of extraordinary interventions: the Troubled Asset Relief Program (TARP), the conservatorship of Fannie Mae and Freddie Mac, the bailout of AIG, the facilitation of emergency mergers, and the Federal Reserve's unprecedented expansion of its balance sheet. These interventions stabilized the financial system and almost certainly prevented a catastrophic economic depression. That is the genuine public benefit argument for them.

The less examined side of the story is who absorbed the losses and who didn't. The major financial institutions that created and sold the toxic mortgage-backed securities that triggered the crisis received government support that allowed most of them to continue operating. Their shareholders took losses significant ones but the institutions survived. The executives who ran them, in many cases, kept their jobs and were eventually rewarded as their institutions recovered. The homeowners who bought houses with loans that shouldn't have been made and are now worth less than the mortgages on them received far less support. The unemployment that resulted from the crisis; the lost jobs, the destroyed savings, the careers that never recovered fell primarily on the people least equipped to absorb it.

This is not an argument against any specific policy decision made in the crucible of the 2008 crisis. Policymakers were making decisions under extraordinary time pressure with incomplete information about what the consequences of alternative paths would be. The point is structural: the financial system is designed, at its deepest level, to protect large concentrations of capital. When those concentrations come under threat, the political and regulatory mechanisms that exist to manage the system activate in ways that, consciously or not, tend to protect the large concentrations first.

An Operator internalizes this not as a reason for anger but as a reason for positioning. If you know that large capital concentrations tend to get bailed out in crises and that asset prices tend to recover while wage income suffers, what does that tell you about the long-term value of building assets rather than depending primarily on labor income? It tells you that the system, whatever its moral complexities, consistently rewards asset ownership. So own assets.

The Tax Code Architecture

The United States Internal Revenue Code is approximately 7,000 pages long, with tens of thousands of additional pages of Treasury regulations and IRS guidance. No human being understands all of it. This complexity is not an accident. Complex tax codes benefit those who can afford to hire the expertise to navigate them. Simple tax codes, in contrast, might be more equitable but would eliminate enormous amounts of revenue for accountants, tax attorneys, financial planners, and the lobbying industry that shapes the code's continued evolution.

Here are the structural features of the tax code that an Operator needs to understand at a conceptual level (we will go much deeper in Chapter 7):

First, the distinction between capital income and labor income. In the United States, income from labor; your salary, your wages, your self-employment income is taxed at ordinary income rates, which can reach 37% at the federal level for high earners, plus payroll taxes, plus state income taxes in most states. Income from capital, dividends, long-term capital gains, carried interest is taxed at significantly lower rates, typically 15% or 20% at the federal level for most taxpayers. The tax code treats income you earn by working harder than income you earn by having. This is not an accident. It reflects the political influence of those who earn primarily capital income.

Second, the favorable treatment of debt. Interest paid on business debt is generally deductible. This creates a powerful incentive to use debt in business and investment contexts, which benefits those who have access to capital and credit meaning, those who already have wealth. The deductibility of mortgage interest for homeowners is a politically popular version of the same principle, though its direct benefit flows disproportionately to higher-income homeowners with larger mortgages in higher tax brackets.

Third, depreciation. When a business buys a physical asset equipment, a building, a vehicle - the tax code allows the cost to be deducted from income over time rather than all at once, reflecting the asset's useful life. This is logical. But Congress periodically passes "bonus depreciation" provisions that allow the immediate deduction of a much larger portion of an asset's cost sometimes 100% in the year of purchase. This creates enormous tax advantages for businesses that acquire physical assets, particularly in real estate, where bonus depreciation and cost segregation strategies can generate paper losses that shelter other income. These strategies are legal, available, and almost completely unknown to people who don't own businesses or investment real estate.

Fourth, the stepped-up basis. When you inherit an asset say, shares of stock that your parent purchased for $10,000 that are now worth $100,000 the capital gains tax that would have been owed on the $90,000 appreciation is eliminated. Your tax basis in the asset is "stepped up" to its value at the date of inheritance. You could sell it immediately for

$100,000 and owe zero capital gains tax. This provision, which primarily benefits wealthy estates that hold appreciated assets across generations, costs the federal government tens of billions of dollars per year in foregone revenue. It has survived every legislative attempt to modify it because the estates it benefits are very good at political engagement.

The Operator's relationship to the tax code is neither outrage at its inequities nor passive acceptance of whatever tax bill arrives each April. The Operator studies the tax code with professional guidance and builds a financial structure that takes legal advantage of every provision available. This is what every sophisticated business owner and investor does. The fact that most ordinary people don't do it is a function of lack of knowledge, not lack of opportunity.

The Operator's Tactical Relationship with Regulation

The Operator's relationship with regulation is not adversarial. Regulation creates order, and order creates opportunity. Regulations that establish property rights, enforce contracts, prevent fraud, and ensure market transparency are the foundation upon which every investment and business decision an Operator makes is built. Without them, the whole game collapses into chaos, and in chaos, might makes right and the biggest actor wins which is never you.

But regulation also creates constraints and costs. And an Operator's approach to regulatory constraints is tactical rather than emotional. The question is not "how do I avoid regulation?" because trying to operate outside the legal framework is a path to catastrophe. The question is "how do I structure my operation to comply with the relevant regulations at minimum cost and maximum strategic advantage?"

This means understanding which regulations apply to your situation and which don't. It means knowing when a legal entity structure changes your regulatory exposure. It means understanding when regulatory arbitrage operating in a jurisdiction or through a vehicle that has different regulatory treatment than the default is legal and advantageous. It means staying current, because regulations change and yesterday's optimized structure may be tomorrow's compliance problem.

Most importantly, the Operator cultivates relationships with professionals who live in the regulatory world: tax attorneys, CPAs with industry expertise, securities attorneys, compliance consultants. These are not expenses. They are investments in situational awareness. The cost of not knowing a regulatory development that affects your operation dwarfs any fee you would pay a professional to keep you informed and compliant.

Operator Rule: Regulation Is the Field, Not the Enemy

The Operator does not fight the regulatory environment. The Operator learns it in sufficient depth to navigate it with precision, builds a professional team that stays current with changes, and structures every major decision with regulatory implications in mind from the start rather than retrofitting compliance after the fact. The cost of legal ignorance is always higher than the cost of legal knowledge.

The government is a force in your financial life whether you engage with it or not. The Operator engages with awareness, with strategy, and with the professional support to do it right. The alternative is to be a passive recipient of whatever tax bill, regulatory burden, or policy consequence the system delivers, which is not an Operator outcome.

Chapter 4

The Hidden Hand: Central Banks and Global Capital Flows

"The study of money, above all other fields in economics, is one in which complexity is used to disguise truth or to evade truth, not to reveal it." **John Kenneth Galbraith**

There is a level of the financial world where the headlines on CNBC are not just late, they are irrelevant. At this level, the movements that matter happened days or weeks ago, and what the financial media is reporting now is the echo of decisions made in offices the camera never enters. Understanding this level doesn't require security clearances or insider connections. It requires understanding the institutions and mechanisms that move global capital and learning to read their signals with a practiced eye.

The central institutions here are the Federal Reserve System of the United States, the European Central Bank, and the Bank for International Settlements. There are others, the Bank of Japan, the People's Bank of China, the Bank of England but these three are the axes around which the global financial system rotates. Their decisions determine the price of credit, the value of currencies, the attractiveness of asset classes, and the direction of capital flows across the global economy.

The Fed, the ECB, and the BIS

We have already discussed the Federal Reserve in some depth. Let's add the European Central Bank and the Bank for International Settlements to the picture, because together they paint a more complete portrait of how global monetary policy actually works.

The European Central Bank, established in 1998 to manage monetary policy for the eurozone, has a fundamentally different mandate than the Federal Reserve. The Fed has a "dual mandate" price stability and maximum employment. The ECB's primary mandate is price stability, full stop. This distinction has had enormous practical consequences. In the years following the 2008 financial crisis, the Fed moved aggressively to stimulate the economy through quantitative easing and near-zero interest rates. The ECB was slower to adopt similar measures, in part because of political constraints within the eurozone particularly the influence of German economic orthodoxy, which historically views central bank money creation with deep suspicion rooted in the hyperinflation of the Weimar

Republic. This divergence in policy contributed to the eurozone's more prolonged economic stagnation in the 2010s relative to the United States.

The Bank for International Settlements is the least well-known of the three but arguably the most important from a global systems perspective. The BIS, headquartered in Basel, Switzerland, is often described as "the central bank for central banks." It provides banking services to the world's major central banks, facilitates cooperation among them, and serves as a forum for monetary policy discussion. The BIS also sets the global banking regulatory standards, the Basel Accords that determine how much capital banks worldwide must hold against their assets. The Basel III framework, developed in response to the 2008 financial crisis, requires banks to hold higher levels of high-quality capital, which has affected lending behavior globally and contributed to the growth of "shadow banking" credit intermediation by non-bank entities that are less subject to these capital requirements.

The Operator's interest in these institutions is practical, not academic. Their decisions create the macro environment within which every investment decision plays out. When the Fed signals a change in the direction of interest rates,

Operators who understand the implications can position accordingly, not on inside information (which would be illegal), but on publicly available signals that most market participants either don't read or don't understand.

How Rate Decisions Move Markets Before You Know

The conventional narrative is that the Fed makes interest rate decisions and then markets react. This narrative is true in a narrow, mechanical sense, the federal funds rate changes when the Federal Open Market Committee votes to change it but it misses the larger reality: sophisticated market participants are pricing expected future rate changes into assets continuously, long before any official announcement.

The Fed, to its credit, has become increasingly transparent over the past two decades in an effort to reduce market volatility from unexpected policy changes. The "dot plot" a chart showing each FOMC member's projection for the future path of interest rates is published quarterly. FOMC minutes are published three weeks after each meeting. Federal Reserve officials give speeches constantly, and the financial press dissects every word for policy signals. The Fed Funds futures market prices the probability of various rate outcomes at future meetings in real time. By the time the Fed actually changes rates, sophisticated investors have already positioned for it often weeks or months in advance.

This means that for an Operator, the useful information is not the rate decision itself but the trajectory of thinking among Fed officials. Is the Fed more worried about inflation or about employment? Are the economic data coming in stronger or weaker than their models projected? When a Fed governor gives a speech about "anchored inflation expectations" versus "persistent inflationary pressures," these are signals. When the dot plot shows a shift in the median projection for the fed funds rate a year out, that is a signal. When the minutes reveal unexpected disagreement among FOMC members, that is a signal.

Reading these signals requires sustained attention and a working understanding of how rate changes flow through the economy. Here is the transmission mechanism in simplified form: The Fed raises rates. Short-term borrowing costs rise immediately. Longer-term rates, mortgage rates, corporate bond rates tend to follow, though the relationship is not mechanical. Higher mortgage rates reduce the purchasing power of homebuyers, which reduces demand for housing, which puts downward pressure on home prices and residential construction. Higher corporate borrowing costs reduce business investment and profitability, particularly for companies with heavy debt loads. Higher rates make bonds more attractive relative to stocks (since bonds pay more in interest), which tends to draw capital from equities into fixed income, putting downward pressure on stock prices. The dollar tends to strengthen as higher US rates attract foreign capital seeking yield, which makes US exports more expensive and imports cheaper, affecting trade balances and multinational corporate earnings.

Each link in this chain creates implications for specific investment decisions. Real estate in a rising rate environment faces headwinds from reduced affordability. Highly indebted companies face higher refinancing costs. Growth stocks, whose value depends heavily on distant future earnings discounted back to the present, are particularly sensitive to rate increases. Dividend-paying value stocks, with cash flows more certain and near-term, hold up better. Financial companies like banks and insurance companies often benefit from rising rates because their net interest margins expand.

The Operator does not wait for these dynamics to become obvious in headlines. The Operator positions ahead of the cycle, reducing exposure to rate-sensitive assets before the cycle turns, adding to them when the cycle turns the other direction.

Sovereign Wealth Funds and Institutional Money Flows

There is another category of global capital that most retail investors don't think about but that exerts enormous influence on asset prices: sovereign wealth funds. These are investment funds owned and operated by national governments, typically funded by commodity revenues (oil is the most common source) or accumulated trade surpluses. The largest Norway's Government Pension Fund Global, the Abu Dhabi Investment Authority, China's China Investment Corporation, Saudi Arabia's Public Investment Fund manage trillions of dollars in assets.

Sovereign wealth funds are significant for several reasons. First, their scale: when a fund managing $1 trillion decides to allocate more capital to a particular asset class, the flows are large enough to move prices meaningfully. Second, their time horizon: these funds are managing money on behalf of future generations of citizens, which means they can maintain positions through volatility that would force shorter-term investors to sell. Third, their growing ambition: sovereign wealth funds that once invested primarily in listed equities and bonds have expanded into private equity, real estate, infrastructure, and direct investments in companies. They are becoming more like private equity firms than passive investors.

For an Operator, the practical relevance of sovereign wealth funds is this: when a major SWF announces a significant allocation to a sector or geography, it is a meaningful signal about where long-term, patient capital is flowing. Norway's fund publishing its equity allocation, the Saudi PIF announcing a major investment in an asset class, the Singapore funds making a move in private credit; these are signals worth noting. They won't always be right, but they represent the considered, long-term view of professional managers with time horizons measured in decades.

What Operators Watch That CNBC Never Covers

Let's be specific about the signals sophisticated operators actually monitor versus the noise that fills financial media.

The yield curve, the relationship between short-term and long-term interest rates is one of the most reliable macro indicators in the financial toolkit. When long-term rates are higher than short-term rates (a normal, "upward-sloping" yield curve), the economy is generally in expansion. When short-term rates rise above long-term rates, a "yield curve inversion" it has historically preceded recessions with remarkable consistency. Every recession in the United States over the past fifty years has been preceded by a yield curve inversion. Not every inversion produces a recession immediately, and the lag time varies, but the signal is worth taking seriously. CNBC covers yield curve inversions when they happen. Operators have been watching the curve every day long before the inversion occurs.

The credit spread, the difference in yield between corporate bonds (particularly high-yield, or "junk" bonds) and comparable Treasury securities is a real-time measure of the market's risk appetite. When credit spreads are narrow, investors are comfortable accepting less yield premium to hold riskier bonds, which signals confidence in the economic outlook. When spreads widen sharply, it signals stress in credit markets, a sign that investors are becoming risk-averse, often ahead of broader market declines. Credit spreads widened dramatically in early 2020 before equity markets had fully priced the pandemic, providing an early warning to those who were watching.

The TED spread; the difference between the rate on three-month Eurodollar deposits and three-month Treasury bills measures banking system stress. When banks don't trust each other enough to lend, the TED spread widens. It spiked to unprecedented levels in late 2008 as the interbank lending market froze. Watching the TED spread is watching the pulse of the banking system.

Global shipping rates particularly the Baltic Dry Index, which tracks the cost of shipping dry bulk commodities like coal, grain, and iron ore are a leading indicator of global economic activity. You can't fake shipping rates. When demand for commodities rises, shipping rates rise. When the global economy slows, shipping capacity exceeds demand and rates fall. Watching shipping rates gives you a real-time window into global trade flows that precedes the official economic data by weeks.

Currency dynamics, particularly the dollar index (DXY), which measures the US dollar against a basket of major currencies, affect everything. A strong dollar is generally good for US consumers (imports are cheaper) and bad for US multinationals (overseas earnings translate back to fewer dollars) and emerging market economies (which often have debts denominated in dollars that become more expensive to service as the dollar strengthens). A weak dollar is the inverse. The dollar's direction is a macro input into dozens of other investment decisions.

These are the signals Operators monitor. Not because any one of them is a reliable crystal ball, none of them is but because taken together, they provide a macro picture that is far richer and more current than anything on a financial news broadcast. The Operator who understands what these signals mean and watches them consistently has an informational advantage over the vast majority of retail investors who wait for the news to tell them what already happened.

The Operator's Macro Dashboard

Build a simple macro monitoring routine. Weekly or monthly, check: the yield curve shape (2-year vs. 10-year Treasury spread), credit spreads (high-yield spreads via any financial data provider), the dollar index, commodity prices (oil, gold, copper), and the Fed's communication calendar. This takes twenty minutes and provides a macro context for every investment decision you make. Most retail investors never look at any of these. You now will.

The global financial system is not chaos. It is a complex machine with identifiable mechanisms and legible signals. The challenge is that most of those signals are in a language, the language of financial mechanics, credit dynamics, and monetary policy that is never taught to ordinary people. Part One of this book has been an intensive language course. By now, you can read more of that language than the vast majority of the population. The rest of this book is about what you do with that literacy.

PART TWO:

The Operator's Global Toolkit

Chapter 5

International Markets and Why You Should Care

"The world is interconnected in ways that most investors have not yet internalized. To invest only in what you can see from your front door is to leave half the opportunity on the table."
The Operator's Creed

Most Americans invest as if the rest of the world doesn't exist. This is understandable, the US market is the largest, most liquid, most transparent financial market in the world. The S&P 500 contains some of the most dynamic and profitable companies in human history. American investors have been rewarded, particularly in the decade following 2010, for their home country bias. Why look elsewhere when home is working so well?

Because the world changes. Because home bias is a cognitive distortion, not a strategy. Because the next decade of outperformance may not belong to the same geography as the last. And because a truly global Operator understands that diversifying across geographies, currencies, and economic cycles is not just about managing risk, it is about accessing opportunity that simply doesn't exist within any single national market.

How Global Markets Are Interconnected

The first thing to understand about international investing is that "international markets" is not a monolith. The world's equity markets can be roughly segmented into three categories: developed markets, emerging markets, and frontier markets. Each has different risk and return characteristics, different liquidity profiles, and different drivers.

Developed markets include the United States, Canada, Western Europe, Japan, Australia, and a handful of others. These markets are characterized by strong institutional frameworks, liquid securities markets, relatively transparent corporate governance, and stable currencies (with the occasional significant exception). The correlation between developed market returns has increased significantly over the past twenty years as capital flows have become more global meaning that when the US market sells off sharply, European and Japanese markets tend to sell off too, which limits the diversification benefit of simply moving money from US stocks to European or Japanese stocks.

Emerging markets include China, India, Brazil, South Korea, Taiwan, Mexico, South Africa, Indonesia, and dozens of others. These markets are characterized by higher growth potential emerging economies are often growing faster than developed ones but also higher volatility, less developed institutional frameworks, greater currency risk, and more political risk. The MSCI Emerging Markets Index has had periods of extraordinary outperformance relative to developed markets and periods of significant underperformance. The key is that emerging market returns are not perfectly correlated with US market returns, which means they genuinely add diversification to a portfolio, particularly over long time periods.

Frontier markets are the smaller, less developed markets Vietnam, Nigeria, Bangladesh, Kenya, Sri Lanka, and others. These are higher-risk, lower-liquidity markets with even greater potential for asymmetric returns and greater potential for catastrophic outcomes. Most Operators outside of specialized emerging market funds will have minimal or no direct exposure to frontier markets, but understanding they exist and that they represent the leading edge of global economic development is part of the global Operator's awareness.

The interconnectedness of global markets operates through several channels. Capital flows: when institutional investors globally reduce risk appetite, they pull capital from emerging markets to safe havens (typically US Treasuries and the dollar), which causes emerging market currencies to weaken, interest rates to rise, and stock prices to fall. Trade flows: a slowdown in Chinese manufacturing reduces demand for Australian iron ore, which reduces Australian export revenues, which affects the Australian dollar and Australian equities. Currency channels: when the dollar strengthens, it puts pressure on commodities priced in dollars (which become more expensive for non-dollar buyers) and on emerging market borrowers with dollar-denominated debt. Sentiment channels: when a major developed market suffers a shock, a financial crisis, a geopolitical event; the resulting risk aversion tends to spread globally, at least initially.

Currency Dynamics and How They Affect Every Investment

Here is something most retail investors learn too late: every international investment is actually two investments. You are investing in the asset itself the stocks, bonds, or real estate of a foreign country and you are simultaneously investing in the currency of that country relative to your home currency. These two investments can work for you simultaneously, against you simultaneously, or in opposite directions. Understanding which is which at any given time is essential.

Let's take a concrete example. Suppose you invest $10,000 in a Brazilian stock fund when the exchange rate is 5 Brazilian reals per US dollar. A year later, the Brazilian stocks you've invested in have risen 15% in local currency terms a strong return. But over that same year, the Brazilian real has weakened from 5 to 6 per dollar, a 17% depreciation. When you convert your 15% gain in reals back to dollars, you've actually lost money. The currency moves more than offset the equity gain.

This example is not hypothetical. Currency moves of this magnitude or larger are common in emerging market contexts. The Brazilian real, the South African rand, the Turkish lira, the Argentine peso these currencies have experienced enormous volatility over the past decade. Operators who invest in emerging markets without understanding currency dynamics are flying blind.

Currency management strategies include hedging using currency forwards or options to lock in exchange rates and currency diversification, the deliberate maintenance of assets in multiple currencies so that no single currency move causes catastrophic damage. For most individual Operators, sophisticated currency hedging is neither practical nor cost-effective. What is practical is building a general awareness of currency trends and sizing emerging market positions appropriately given the additional risk layer.

The US dollar's global dominance also means that dollar movements affect even domestic investments. When the dollar weakens, commodity prices which are globally priced in dollars tend to rise in dollar terms, benefiting commodity producers. When the dollar strengthens, US multinationals reporting earnings in dollars take a hit on their overseas revenues. An Operator who understands dollar dynamics has a macro lens that helps interpret earnings reports, commodity prices, and emerging market performance simultaneously.

Emerging Markets: Risk, Reward, and Asymmetry

The investment case for emerging markets rests on a few durable foundations. First, growth: emerging economies particularly India, Southeast Asia, and parts of Africa are at earlier stages of economic development, with larger potential for growth driven by urbanization, technology adoption, rising middle-class consumption, and catch-up productivity. Second, demographics: many emerging markets have younger populations than developed markets, which typically supports economic growth and consumption. Third, valuation: emerging market equities have, at various points, traded at significant discounts to developed market peers on standard valuation metrics, creating the potential for mean reversion gains on top of underlying economic growth.

The risks are equally real. Political risk - the risk that a change of government, a policy reversal, or a geopolitical event dramatically changes the investment landscape is substantially higher in emerging markets. Governance risk - the risk that corporate management acts against the interests of minority shareholders is higher. Liquidity risk - the risk that markets become illiquid during stress periods is higher. Currency risk, as discussed, is substantial. And information quality varies significantly, financial reporting in emerging markets can be less reliable than in developed markets, making fundamental analysis more difficult and valuation more uncertain.

The Operator's approach to emerging markets: treat them as a return-enhancing, volatility-adding sleeve in a diversified portfolio not the core. A 10-20% allocation to global equities including emerging markets, accessed through low-cost diversified funds, provides meaningful diversification and growth exposure without concentrating risk in any single emerging market. For Operators with specific expertise in a region or sector perhaps someone who has worked in Southeast Asia or has deep knowledge of the technology sector in India more concentrated positions can be appropriate, but they should be sized with the additional risk in mind.

Building a Geographically Diversified Operator Portfolio

The standard institutional approach to global equity allocation begins with a benchmark most commonly the MSCI All Country World Index (ACWI), which covers approximately 47 countries across developed and emerging markets. This benchmark is roughly 60% US equities, with the remaining 40% spread across international developed and emerging markets. Many institutional investors pension funds, endowments use this as a starting point and then adjust based on their views and constraints.

For an individual Operator, the relevant question is not "how do I replicate an institutional benchmark?" but "what global exposure serves my specific financial situation, time horizon, and risk tolerance?" Here is a framework for thinking about it:

The core 50-70% of your equity exposure should be in markets and securities you understand well and can monitor effectively. For most US-based Operators, this will be primarily US equities. This is not an endorsement of home bias; it is a recognition that you are more likely to make good decisions in markets you understand than in markets you don't.

The developed international sleeve 15-25% provides exposure to economies and industries not well represented in the US market. European luxury goods, Japanese precision manufacturing, Canadian financial services, Australian resources these are sectors where non-US developed markets may have structural advantages. Low-cost index funds or ETFs tracking developed international markets are the most efficient access vehicles for most Operators.

The emerging markets sleeve 10-20% provides growth exposure and genuine diversification. Again, broad index exposure through low-cost ETFs is the most practical approach unless you have specific regional expertise.

Beyond equities, global diversification extends to other asset classes: international real estate investment trusts, global bond exposure (with currency considerations carefully managed), international commodity exposure, and for sophisticated Operators, direct investment in foreign real estate or businesses. Each of these deserves individual evaluation based on the Operator's specific situation.

OPERATOR PRINCIPLE: HOME BIAS IS A COGNITIVE ERROR, NOT A STRATEGY

Every investor has a natural preference for familiar markets. The Operator acknowledges this preference as a psychological artifact and corrects for it deliberately. The global economy contains dozens of markets, hundreds of sectors, and thousands of companies. The greatest investment opportunity of the next decade may be in a country you've never visited, in an industry you don't currently follow. Build the exposure now, while it's cheap, and before the opportunity is obvious to everyone.

The world is the Operator's marketplace. Every country is a potential investment. Every currency is a potential tool. Every global economic trend is a potential opportunity. The Operator who has built genuine global awareness — who watches global markets, understands currency dynamics, and has at least some exposure to international growth — is operating with a far wider field of view than the investor who only owns US stocks. And in investing, as in any other domain where information is an advantage, field of view is everything.

Chapter 6

Offshore Structures: Legal, Ethical, and Strategic

"The rich do not hide their money offshore because they are criminals. They do it because the system permits it, and because it works. The question is not whether it's available to you — it is whether you know enough to use it correctly." **The Operator's Creed**

Critical Disclaimer

Everything in this chapter describes legal structures and strategies used by sophisticated individuals and businesses worldwide. Nothing in this chapter constitutes legal or tax advice. International tax and legal compliance is extraordinarily complex and varies by individual circumstance, citizenship, residency, and applicable law. Before implementing any offshore structure, you must consult a qualified international tax attorney and a CPA with specific international tax expertise. Failure to comply with US reporting requirements for foreign accounts and structures FBAR, FATCA, and other regulations carries severe civil and criminal penalties. This chapter is educational. The professionals you hire will provide the specifics that apply to your situation.

Few financial topics generate more mythology, suspicion, and confusion than offshore banking and international structures. In the popular imagination, offshore accounts belong to criminals, tax cheats, and Bond villains. In reality, they are legal tools used by millions of businesses and individuals worldwide for entirely legitimate purposes: international business operations, asset protection, estate planning, currency diversification, and legal tax optimization within the framework of applicable law.

The Operator's job is to separate the myth from the reality, understand what these structures actually do, and make informed decisions about whether and how they apply to their situation.

What Offshore Banking and Structures Actually Are

An "offshore" account or structure is simply one that exists in a jurisdiction different from your home country. For a US citizen, a bank account in Switzerland, an LLC formed in the Cayman Islands, or a trust established under the laws of the British Virgin Islands is "offshore." The term carries a negative connotation that is largely unjustified in the context of legal, properly reported structures.

The jurisdictions most commonly used for international structures each have specific legal and tax characteristics that make them useful for particular purposes. Switzerland has traditionally been favored for banking privacy and the stability of the Swiss franc. The Cayman Islands are the dominant domicile for hedge funds because of their regulatory framework and tax neutrality. The British Virgin Islands are widely used for holding companies because of their flexibility, low cost, and established legal framework. Singapore and Hong Kong have become increasingly important as international financial centers for Asia-Pacific operations. Smaller jurisdictions like Belize, Nevis, and the Cook Islands have niche uses primarily in asset protection contexts.

It's critical to understand that "offshore" does not mean "secret from the IRS." For US citizens and permanent residents, foreign financial accounts and structures must be reported to the IRS and FinCEN under a comprehensive framework of disclosure requirements. The Foreign Account Tax Compliance Act (FATCA) requires foreign financial institutions to report accounts held by US persons to the IRS. The Foreign Bank Account Report (FBAR) requires US persons to file annual reports with FinCEN disclosing foreign accounts above $10,000. Form 8938 requires disclosure of specified foreign financial assets above various thresholds. Failure to comply with these requirements is not a gray area, it is a serious federal crime with civil penalties up to $100,000 per violation and potential criminal prosecution.

The era of truly "secret" offshore accounts, the kind you open in Geneva, tell no one about, and never report effectively ended with the passage of FATCA in 2010 and the subsequent adoption of the Common Reporting Standard by most major financial jurisdictions globally. Today, financial institutions in almost every major offshore jurisdiction automatically share account information with the home country tax authorities of their account holders. The days of using offshore accounts to hide income are not just legally dangerous, they are largely operationally impossible at any reputable institution.

Legal Uses of International Accounts, Trusts, and Holding Companies

With that foundational clarity established, let's look at what offshore structures actually do in legitimate use cases.

International business operations. If you operate a business that has customers, suppliers, contractors, or employees in multiple countries, an international holding structure is not a tax dodge, it is a practical operational tool. A company operating across three or four countries may have legitimate reasons to structure its international operations through a holding company in a jurisdiction with a favorable tax treaty network, clear corporate law, and simple regulations. This is standard practice for any international business of meaningful scale. The goal is not to hide from taxes but to avoid paying tax multiple times on the same income across multiple jurisdictions what tax professionals call "double taxation."

Asset protection. Certain offshore jurisdictions have trust and corporate laws that make them useful for asset protection specifically, protection against future creditors. This is entirely legal when done properly and proactively (not as a fraudulent transfer after a claim has been made). An offshore asset protection trust in a jurisdiction with short statutes of limitations for fraudulent transfer claims, charging order protection, and strong creditor barriers can provide meaningful protection for assets that might otherwise be vulnerable to US civil judgments. Medical professionals, business owners in high-liability industries, and others with significant creditor risk are the primary users of these structures.

Currency and banking diversification. Holding accounts in multiple currencies at banks in multiple jurisdictions protects against the scenario in which a single banking system fails or a single currency experiences severe devaluation. This is not a paranoid concern; it is the kind of risk management that sophisticated individuals and businesses have practiced for centuries. Argentinians who held dollar accounts offshore survived the 2001-2002 peso collapse with their wealth largely intact. Those who held only pesos suffered devastating losses. Diversification applies to banking systems, not just investment portfolios.

Estate planning. International trusts and structures can be powerful estate planning tools, particularly for families with assets or beneficiaries in multiple countries. They can facilitate the orderly transfer of wealth across generations and across jurisdictions in a way that minimizes probate complexity and potential conflicts between different countries' inheritance laws.

Why the Ultra-Wealthy Use Multiple Jurisdictions

The ultra-wealthy the families and individuals at the very top of the global wealth distribution routinely maintain presences in multiple jurisdictions: homes, businesses, investments, legal structures, and sometimes residency or citizenship in multiple countries. This is not about evading obligations. It is about operating in a genuinely global context where no single jurisdiction has a claim to the entirety of a global operation.

The concept of "second citizenship" or "residence by investment" programs has grown significantly. Countries including Portugal, Malta, St. Kitts and Nevis, Dominica, Vanuatu, and others offer citizenship or long-term residency in exchange for investments in real estate, government bonds, or direct contributions to national development funds. These programs are legal, heavily regulated, and used by wealthy individuals worldwide for a variety of reasons: travel freedom (a US passport, while powerful, doesn't provide visa-free access to every desirable destination), business flexibility (operating under a different flag can simplify certain international transactions), and contingency planning (having a legal right to reside in another country provides optionality in uncertain times).

For US citizens, there is an important wrinkle: the United States taxes its citizens on worldwide income regardless of where they live. A US citizen living in Singapore and earning income entirely from Singapore sources still owes US taxes (subject to the Foreign Earned Income Exclusion and Foreign Tax Credit). This means that for most US citizens, the tax optimization benefits of offshore structures are more limited than for citizens of most other developed countries, whose governments tax on a residency basis rather than a citizenship basis. The only way for a US citizen to fully escape US worldwide taxation is to renounce citizenship, a drastic, irreversible step with its own tax consequences (the "exit tax") that very few people should consider, and then only with extensive legal counsel.

What an Operator at Various Wealth Levels Can Realistically Consider

Let's be direct about scale and practicality. Offshore structures carry setup costs, annual maintenance costs, compliance costs, and complexity that make them impractical and economically irrational below certain asset levels.

At under $500,000 in net worth, offshore structures are almost certainly not cost-effective. The compliance costs attorney fees, accounting fees, annual maintenance can easily run $5,000-$15,000 per year or more. At this wealth level, the focus should be on building the operation domestically.

At $500,000 to $2 million, the primary relevant consideration might be a foreign bank account for genuine currency diversification or international business operations. Simple, transparent, properly reported. This is not expensive or complex.

At $2 million to $10 million, an international holding structure for business operations, or an offshore asset protection trust for high-liability professionals, may begin to make economic sense. The cost-benefit analysis depends heavily on the nature of the business and the specific liability profile.

Above $10 million, the full range of international structures holding companies, trusts, multi-jurisdiction banking is worth serious exploration with qualified international tax counsel. The complexity is manageable with the right professional team, and the potential benefits in asset protection, estate planning efficiency, and legal tax optimization can be substantial.

At every level, the non-negotiable requirement is full compliance with all reporting requirements. An offshore structure that isn't properly disclosed is not a sophisticated financial strategy. It is a criminal exposure. Any advisor who suggests you don't need to report a foreign account or structure should be immediately dismissed and possibly reported to the IRS.

THE THREE QUESTIONS FOR ANY OFFSHORE STRUCTURE

1. ***Is there a legitimate, non-tax-avoidance business or personal purpose? (Business operations, asset protection, currency diversification, estate planning - all legitimate.)***
2. ***Will it be fully disclosed and compliant with all applicable US reporting requirements?***
3. ***Has a qualified international tax attorney reviewed and signed off on the structure and the ongoing compliance obligations? If the answer to any of these is "no," do not proceed.***

Offshore structures are tools. Like all tools, they can be used well or badly. Used well legally, transparently, for legitimate purposes, they are part of the toolkit that separates an Operator's financial architecture from a civilian's. Used badly as vehicles for concealment, as schemes to avoid legitimate tax obligations, they are paths to penalties and prosecution that can undo everything you've built. The Operator chooses the former, exclusively.

Chapter 7

Tax Strategy at the Operator Level

"The hardest thing in the world to understand is the income tax."

Albert Einstein (attributed)

Disclaimer

Nothing in this chapter constitutes tax advice. Tax law is complex, changes frequently, and varies by individual circumstance. All strategies discussed here are general concepts. Consult a qualified CPA and tax attorney before implementing any tax strategy. The goal of this chapter is to give you the conceptual framework to have intelligent conversations with your tax professionals, not to replace them.

Taxes are the largest single expense in the financial life of most Operators larger than housing, larger than food, larger than any investment you will ever make. Yet most people spend more time optimizing their Netflix subscription than they spend thinking strategically about their tax situation. This is a catastrophic misallocation of attention.

The distinction every Operator must internalize from the start: tax evasion is illegal and will end your operation. Tax optimization is legal, explicitly permitted, and actively practiced by every sophisticated business owner and investor in the world. The difference between these two things is not a matter of degree, it is a bright legal line. Tax evasion involves concealing income, falsifying records, or otherwise deceiving tax authorities. Tax optimization involves using the provisions of the existing tax code as Congress wrote them and the IRS enforces them to legally reduce your tax liability. The Supreme Court has repeatedly affirmed that you have no legal obligation to pay more taxes than the law requires.

The Operator pays every dollar of tax legally owed and not one cent more. Getting to "not one cent more" requires understanding the tools available.

The Difference between Evasion and Optimization

Let's make this concrete with a few examples of the line between legal and illegal.

Tax evasion: receiving $50,000 in cash income and not reporting it on your tax return. Illegal straightforwardly fraud.

Tax optimization: structuring a business as an S-corporation, taking a "reasonable salary," and receiving the remaining business income as a distribution that is not subject to self-employment taxes. Completely legal widely practiced worth potentially thousands of dollars per year in tax savings.

Tax evasion: claiming personal expenses as business deductions your personal car, your family vacation, your children's tuition without genuine business purpose.

Tax optimization: documenting legitimate business use of a vehicle, deducting the business-use percentage of operating costs, and potentially using Section 179 or bonus depreciation to immediately expense a significant portion of the vehicle's purchase price against business income.

The line is bright. The Operator never approaches it, because the downside of crossing it back taxes, penalties, interest, potential criminal prosecution, reputational destruction is catastrophically asymmetric relative to any short-term tax saving. Tax optimization should feel comfortable, defensible, and transparent. If a strategy requires concealment or explanation that you wouldn't want to make in front of a tax court judge, it's on the wrong side of the line.

Depreciation, Cost Segregation, and Real Estate

Real estate is the most tax-advantaged asset class in the United States. Period. The combination of depreciation, leverage, and favorable capital gains treatment makes it uniquely powerful from a tax perspective, and understanding why is essential for any Operator who either has or is considering real estate investments.

Depreciation is the tax code's acknowledgment that physical assets wear out over time. For residential rental property, the IRS allows the building structure (not the land - land doesn't depreciate) to be deducted over 27.5 years. For commercial property, the depreciation period is 39 years. This creates a "paper loss" a deduction that reduces taxable income without requiring an actual cash outflow. A $275,000 rental property (ignoring land value) generates approximately $10,000 per year in depreciation deductions. If the property generates $12,000 in rental income against $10,000 in cash expenses, the taxable income is only $2,000 not $12,000 despite the property generating positive cash flow. The depreciation deduction sheltered $10,000 of income from tax.

Cost segregation takes this further. A cost segregation study performed by engineers and accountants reclassifies components of a real estate purchase from the standard 27.5-year or 39-year depreciation schedules to much shorter categories: 5-year, 7-year, and 15-year property. The components of a building, flooring, lighting, landscaping, parking lots, certain fixtures can be segregated from the structural elements and depreciated much more quickly. Combined with bonus depreciation (which has allowed immediate deduction of 100% of certain assets in recent years, though the specific rules change frequently), a cost segregation study can generate substantial first-year depreciation deductions that significantly reduce or eliminate taxable income from a property in the year of purchase.

Real estate professional status is a tax classification that allows a person who meets certain time-commitment tests to deduct real estate losses (including depreciation losses) against other types of income; wages, investment income, business income rather than being limited to passive loss rules. For a high-income earner who also owns real estate, achieving real estate professional status (or being married to a spouse who qualifies) can create six-figure tax deductions annually. The requirements are specific and must be carefully documented; this is an area where proper professional guidance is not optional.

Opportunity Zones and 1031 Exchanges

The 1031 exchange named for Section 1031 of the Internal Revenue Code is one of the most powerful tax deferral tools available to real estate investors. It allows you to sell an investment property and defer the capital gains tax by rolling the proceeds into a "like-kind" replacement property within specific time limits (45 days to identify the replacement, 180 days to close). Properly executed, 1031 exchanges allow you to grow a real estate portfolio by continuously rolling gains forward essentially interest-free loans from the government potentially deferring the capital gains tax indefinitely. If you hold properties until death, the stepped-up basis provision may eliminate the deferred tax entirely. This combination 1031 exchanges through life, stepped-up basis at death is one of the most legally powerful wealth transfer mechanisms available to real estate investors.

Opportunity Zones, established by the Tax Cuts and Jobs Act of 2017, are designated economically distressed communities where investments receive significant tax benefits. By investing capital gains in a Qualified Opportunity Fund that invests in an Opportunity Zone, an investor can defer and potentially reduce the tax on those gains, and if the investment is held for at least ten years, may exclude capital gains from the Opportunity Zone investment entirely from taxation. This is a powerful incentive for long-term investment in designated areas if the investment performs well but requires careful due diligence on the underlying investment, which should be evaluated on its own merits independent of the tax benefit.

Qualified Business Income, Pass-Through Structures, and S-Corps

The Tax Cuts and Jobs Act of 2017 introduced Section 199A, the Qualified Business Income (QBI) deduction, which allows owners of "pass-through" businesses sole proprietorships, partnerships, LLCs, and S-corporations to deduct up to 20% of their qualified business income from federal taxable income. For a business owner generating $200,000 in QBI, this can mean a $40,000 deduction, saving potentially $14,800 in federal taxes at the 37% bracket. The rules around QBI are complex there are income thresholds, W-2 wage limitations, and specific industry exclusions that affect eligibility but for qualifying business owners, it is an extraordinarily valuable provision.

The S-corporation structure deserves particular attention for self-employed Operators. As a sole proprietor or single-member LLC taxed as a sole proprietor, your entire net business income is subject to self-employment tax (15.3% on the first roughly $160,000 and 2.9% on amounts above that). By electing S-corp taxation and paying yourself a "reasonable salary" for the services you provide to the business, you pay self-employment taxes (as payroll taxes) only on the salary portion. The remaining business profits pass through to you as distributions not subject to these payroll taxes. For a business generating $200,000 in profits with a $100,000 reasonable salary, the S-corp election could save approximately $7,600 per year in self-employment taxes often more than enough to cover the additional cost of S-corp accounting and compliance.

How to Legally Pay the Least Tax the Government Allows

The Operator's tax strategy is not a single tactic, it is a system. Here are the components of a comprehensive Operator tax system:

Entity optimization: Are you using the right business structure for your income level and business type? Sole proprietor, LLC, S-corp, C-corp - each has different tax treatment, and moving between them as your income grows can produce meaningful savings.

Retirement account maximization: The first dollars saved from taxes should go into tax-advantaged retirement accounts. For self-employed Operators, a Solo 401(k) or SEP-IRA can accommodate very large annual contributions potentially $70,000+ per year providing a dollar-for-dollar reduction in taxable income. If you are not maximizing these before pursuing more sophisticated strategies, start here.

Depreciation acceleration: Own real property or equipment in your business? A cost segregation study and bonus depreciation strategy can create first-year deductions that dramatically reduce or eliminate your tax bill in the year of acquisition.

Charitable giving: Donor-advised funds allow you to make a large charitable contribution in a high-income year, take the full deduction immediately, and then distribute the funds to specific charities over time. Contributing appreciated assets (stocks, real estate) to a DAF avoids capital gains tax entirely while generating a deduction at fair market value.

Tax-loss harvesting: In your investment portfolio, realizing losses on securities that have declined in value and immediately reinvesting in similar (but not identical, to avoid wash sale rules) securities creates tax losses that can offset capital gains or, up to $3,000 per year, ordinary income. Systematically harvested across years, tax-loss harvesting can reduce portfolio tax drag significantly.

Qualified opportunity zones: For large capital gain realizations, a QOZ investment can defer and potentially reduce taxes while providing an investment in a designated community.

Proactive quarterly planning: Tax strategy that happens only in April is inherently reactive and suboptimal. The Operator meets with their CPA quarterly to review income, project year-end tax liability, and identifies opportunities to optimize before December 31 the last date on which most tax-advantaged actions can be taken for the current year.

Operator Tax Principle: Taxes Are Negotiated, Not Imposed

For those who plan, taxes are the result of choices entity structure choices, investment vehicle choices, timing choices, charitable choices. For those who don't plan, taxes are an imposition something that happens to you rather than something you manage. The Operator plans. The difference, over a career, is the difference between building wealth and financing the government's priorities with money that could have been yours.

The single most important action you can take after reading this chapter: schedule a meeting with a CPA who specializes in business and investment tax strategy — not a tax preparer who fills out forms, but a strategist who proactively designs your tax structure. The fee for that consultation will be the best return on investment you make this year.

Chapter 8

Alternative Assets and the Operator Allocation

"Diversification is protection against ignorance. It makes little sense if you know what you are doing." **Warren Buffett**

The institutional investment world the world of endowments, pension funds, sovereign wealth funds, and family offices has known for decades that a portfolio limited to stocks and bonds is a suboptimal construct. The Yale Endowment under David Swensen pioneered the approach of allocating heavily to "alternative" assets - real estate, private equity, natural resources; absolute return strategies that had different risk and return characteristics than public markets. The Yale model generated extraordinary returns for decades and inspired most major institutional investors to broaden their allocations significantly.

For most of that time, individual investors had limited access to alternative assets. Private equity deals required institutional minimums. Direct real estate required capital and expertise. Hedge funds were limited to accredited investors with substantial wealth. The democratization of alternatives through new fund structures, regulatory changes, and technology platforms has begun to change this, making at least some of the institutional toolkit available to Operators at various wealth levels.

Real Assets: Real Estate, Commodities, Farmland, and Timberland

Real assets - physical assets that have intrinsic value independent of any promise or contract have historically served as effective hedges against inflation, which is one of their primary attractions in a period when monetary policy has significantly expanded the money supply.

Real estate remains the most accessible real asset for most Operators. The combination of leverage, depreciation, rental income, and appreciation potential makes it a multi-dimensional return vehicle. Direct ownership of residential or commercial rental property is the most widely practiced form of real estate investing, and it has created more individual millionaires than any other asset class in the United States. Real estate investment trusts (REITs) provide liquid exposure to real estate markets without the operational burden of direct ownership they can be bought and sold like stocks, make liquidity accessible, and provide exposure to commercial real estate sectors (office, industrial, healthcare, data centers) that individual investors couldn't access directly.

Commodities - physical raw materials like oil, natural gas, agricultural products, metals provide inflation protection and diversification from financial assets. Commodity prices tend to move independently of stock and bond prices, particularly over shorter time periods. Investors can access commodities through commodity ETFs (which may hold the physical commodity, futures contracts, or a combination), commodity producer stocks, or, for large-scale operations, direct ownership of mineral rights or producing properties.

Farmland has emerged as one of the most sought-after alternative assets among institutional investors over the past decade. Farmland provides steady income from crops and leases, inflation protection as food prices tend to rise with general inflation, and long-term appreciation driven by finite supply of arable land and growing global food demand. Platforms like AcreTrader and FarmTogether have made farmland investing accessible to accredited investors who previously couldn't participate in this market.

Timberland forests managed for sustainable timber production shares many characteristics with farmland but with a unique feature: trees grow. A timber investor effectively has an asset that increases in both quantity and quality over time, providing what is sometimes called a "biological return" on top of timber sales revenue. Major institutional investors including pension funds have allocated to timberland for decades. Access for individual Operators is improving through specialized funds; though direct timberland investment remains largely an institutional and high-net-worth domain.

Private Equity and Private Credit

Private equity investment in private companies not publicly traded has generated strong long-term returns for institutional investors, though the claims require careful analysis. Private equity returns are difficult to compare directly to public market returns because private equity investments are valued periodically rather than daily, which smooths volatility in ways that may be misleading. The performance data is also subject to survivorship bias the funds that report performances are disproportionately those that have done well.

That said, well-executed private equity strategies particularly in the middle market, where companies are large enough to have real operations but small enough to have been overlooked by large PE firms have generated genuine returns that outpace public markets on a risk-adjusted basis for skilled managers. The key word is "skilled." Private equity is highly execution-dependent; the spread between top-quartile and bottom-quartile private equity returns is enormous, unlike the relatively compressed spread in passive public market investing.

For Operators below the threshold where top private equity funds accept commitments (typically $5-25 million minimum), access routes include Business Development Companies (BDCs), which are publicly traded vehicles that invest in private company debt, and newer platforms that aggregate smaller investor commitments to access institutional-quality private equity and private credit deals.

Private credit lending to private companies outside the banking system has grown dramatically since 2008 as bank regulation tightened and banks retreated from certain lending segments. Private credit funds provide debt financing to mid-sized businesses, generating income (often floating rate) with returns typically in the 8-12% range in recent years. The asset class has become a significant and growing allocation for institutional investors and is increasingly accessible to accredited individual investors through registered closed-end funds and specialty platforms.

Hedge Fund Strategies at Smaller Scale

The Operator who cannot access institutional hedge funds directly can nevertheless implement several hedge fund strategy concepts in their personal portfolio using publicly available instruments.

Long-short equity is perhaps the most widely recognized hedge fund strategy - buying (going long) stocks you expect to outperform and shorting stocks you expect to underperform. For individual investors, this is implementable through a combination of direct long positions and short positions through margin accounts, or through inverse ETFs for the short exposure. The challenge is that short selling requires specific account types, margin approval, and carries unique risks (your loss on a short is theoretically unlimited as a stock rises).

Merger arbitrage - buying the stock of an announced acquisition target at a small discount to the announced deal price and profiting when the deal closes — is implementable at the individual investor level with appropriate due diligence. The return comes from the time value of the deal closing spread (typically a few percentage points over a few months) net of the risk that the deal breaks, in which case the target stock often falls significantly.

Global macro strategies - taking positions in currencies, interest rates, commodities, and equity markets based on macroeconomic analysis are accessible to individual investors through the futures markets, currency ETFs, Treasury ETFs, and sector ETFs. This requires the macroeconomic analysis framework developed in earlier chapters and the risk management discipline discussed in Chapter 9.

Collectibles, Art, Royalties, and Non-Correlated Assets

Beyond the categories already discussed, there is a universe of non-traditional asset classes that sophisticated Operators have used to build wealth and diversification.

Collectibles fine art, vintage wine, rare cars, coins, watches, sports cards have generated strong returns for collectors with genuine expertise. The key caveat is "genuine expertise." Collectibles markets are illiquid, opaque, and highly dependent on trend and taste what is valuable today may be less so in twenty years. For most Operators, collectibles should be limited to areas of genuine personal passion and expertise, not treated as investment vehicles outside that domain. Platforms like Masterworks have begun to democratize access to fine art investing, though the underlying illiquidity and valuation uncertainty remain.

Royalty's income streams derived from intellectual property, music rights, patent licensing, natural resource rights are genuinely non-correlated assets. When the stock market crashes, the royalty stream from a popular song or a pharmaceutical patent continues to flow. Platforms like Royalty Exchange allow investors to bid on royalty streams, and some royalty-focused REITs and funds provide exposure to diversified royalty portfolios. This is a niche but genuinely interesting asset class for Operators willing to do the due diligence.

Building an All-Weather Operator Portfolio

The concept of an "all-weather" portfolio one designed to perform adequately across the full range of economic environments was pioneered by Ray Dalio and Bridgewater Associates. The core insight: different asset classes perform well in different economic environments (growth, recession, inflation, deflation), and a portfolio balanced across these environments will be more robust than one optimized for a single scenario.

The Operator's all-weather framework considers four economic environments: rising growth (favors equities, credit, commodities), falling growth (favors long-duration bonds, gold), rising inflation (favors commodities, TIPS, real estate, gold, short-duration bonds), and falling inflation (favors long bonds, some equities). Holding assets that perform well in each environment, in proportions that reflect the uncertainty about which environment will prevail, creates a portfolio that can survive any weather without catastrophic damage.

The specific allocation that works for any individual Operator depends on their time horizon, liquidity needs, tax situation, and access to various asset classes. A simplified version might look like: 35-40% diversified equities (global), 15-20% real estate (direct or REITs), 10-15% real assets (commodities, TIPS, gold), 15-20% fixed income (mixed duration), and 5-15% alternatives (private credit, private equity, other). Adjust based on your specific circumstances, and revisit annually as both your situation and the macro environment change.

OPERATOR PRINCIPLE: DIVERSIFICATION ACROSS ASSET CLASSES BEATS DIVERSIFICATION WITHIN ASSET CLASSES

Owning 50 different US stocks is not true diversification; they will all fall together in a US market correction. True diversification crosses asset classes with genuinely different risk drivers: equities, real estate, real assets, private credit, and alternatives. Build your portfolio so that no single economic environment destroys it. Your goal is not the maximum return, it is the optimal return for the risk you can actually sustain without panic-selling at the worst moment.

Chapter 9

Leverage: The Most Dangerous and Most Powerful Tool

"Give me a lever long enough and a fulcrum on which to place it, and I shall move the world." **Archimedes**

Archimedes was talking about physics. He was also, unknowingly, describing the essence of financial leverage. A lever multiplies force. Financial leverage multiplies outcome in both directions. It accelerates gains with the same mechanical indifference with which it accelerates losses. Understanding this tool its mechanics, its limits, and the psychological demands it places on its user is essential for any Operator who intends to build wealth at scale.

Almost all large-scale wealth in the modern world involves leverage. Real estate investors borrow against properties. Business builders borrow to fund growth. Hedge fund managers use margin to amplify position sizes. The institutions themselves banks, insurance companies, private equity firms operate with leverage ratios that would horrify an individual investor. Leverage is not the villain in the wealth-building story. It is the protagonist's most powerful tool and the one that kills the protagonist most often when mishandled.

Understanding Leverage: Margin, Options, Real Estate, and Business Debt

Leverage takes different forms in different contexts. Understanding each form; its mechanics and its specific risks is the foundation of using it well.

Margin debt is borrowed money from your brokerage firm to purchase securities. If you have $100,000 in your brokerage account, your broker may allow you to borrow an additional $100,000 2:1 leverage to purchase $200,000 in securities. If those securities rise 10%, your gain is $20,000 a 20% return on your original capital. If those securities fall 10%, your loss is $20,000 also a 20% loss of your original capital plus the interest on the borrowed $100,000. If they fall 25%, you're down 50% and may face a margin call requiring you to sell securities or deposit additional funds. If they fall 50%, your equity is wiped out. Margin debt amplifies outcome with brutal, symmetric efficiency.

Options are leveraged financial instruments that give you the right (but not the obligation) to buy or sell an asset at a predetermined price within a specified time period. A call option on a stock gives you the right to buy 100 shares at the "strike" price regardless of where the market price goes. Because options control 100 shares for a fraction of the cost of buying 100 shares outright, they are inherently leveraged. A stock rising 10% might cause an at-the-money call option on that stock to rise 50-100%. Conversely, time decay (the option loses value as its expiration approaches), and the wrong price move, can cause the option to expire worthless a 100% loss of the premium paid. Options are sophisticated instruments that require dedicated study before use.

Real estate leverage is the most widely practiced form of investment leverage and, in many ways, the most forgiving with important caveats. When you buy a $500,000 property with $100,000 down and a $400,000 mortgage, you are operating at 5:1 leverage on your equity. If the property appreciates 10% to $550,000, your $100,000 equity has become $150,000, a 50% return on your invested capital. The mortgage interest is deductible. The cash flow (if positive) services the debt. The depreciation shelters income. Real estate leverage is powerful precisely because it is patient, a thirty-year mortgage doesn't make a margin call. As long as you can service the debt from income (the property's rental income or your other income), temporary price declines do not force you to sell at a loss.

Business debt borrowed money used to fund business operations and growth is the leverage that builds empires. When a business can generate returns on capital higher than its borrowing cost, debt accelerates wealth creation. A business earning 20% returns on its capital, funded partially by debt costing 7%, creates significant value for its equity owners. The critical risk: businesses have operating leverage too fixed costs that must be paid regardless of revenue which amplifies the pain when revenue falls. A business that carries debt *and* has high fixed costs faces a double squeeze in a downturn that can be fatal.

When Leverage Accelerates Wealth vs. When It Destroys It

The determinants of whether leverage helps or hurts come down to a few key variables:

The return on the asset versus the cost of the debt. If your leveraged asset generates returns meaningfully above the cost of borrowing, leverage adds value. If returns are below borrowing cost or if the asset is producing no return at all (such as speculative leverage in a stock that isn't generating earnings) leverage is destroying value continuously through interest cost.

The stability and predictability of the asset's cash flows. Real estate with reliable tenants and long leases can service significant leverage because cash flows are predictable. A highly cyclical business one whose revenue can fall 50% in a recession should carry far less debt, because the same revenue decline that a debt-free business can survive may push a heavily leveraged business into default.

The duration of the debt. Short-term debt that must be refinanced is always more dangerous than long-term fixed-rate debt. The 2008 financial crisis was fundamentally a crisis of short-term financing disappearing: institutions that had borrowed short-term to fund long-term illiquid assets suddenly couldn't roll their debt. The resulting forced selling destroyed trillions in value. A thirty-year fixed-rate mortgage is, in leverage terms, dramatically less dangerous than a short-term commercial loan or a margin account, which the broker can call at any time.

The volatility of the asset's price. An asset that can lose 50% of its value in a normal market cycle (small cap stocks, some commodities, cryptocurrency) should not be financed with significant leverage unless you have the financial resources and psychological fortitude to survive that decline without forced selling. An asset that historically holds its value well stable residential real estate in a strong market, for instance, can sustain higher leverage.

The Operator's Leverage Rules

These are not suggestions. They are the guardrails that separate Operators who build lasting wealth from those who build impressive looking structures that collapse under stress.

Rule 1: Never bet the operation. No single leveraged position should have the capacity to wipe out your entire net worth or your operating cash flow. Size leverage so that a worst-case outcome a 50% decline in the leveraged asset, a total loss is painful but survivable. Your operation, your income-generating capacity, your core assets, your financial foundation must survive every loss scenario you can construct.

Rule 2: Match debt duration to asset duration. Finance long-term assets with long-term debt. Finance short-term assets with short-term debt. Never finance a long-term illiquid asset with short-term debt that must be rolled. This is the mistake that has killed more leveraged operations than any other.

Rule 3: Conservative underwriting beats optimistic underwriting every time. When modeling whether you can afford to carry a leveraged position or whether a property, a business, or an investment use conservative assumptions. What does the cash flow look like if occupancy is 80% instead of 95%? What does it look like if revenue falls 25%? If the position doesn't work under conservative assumptions, it doesn't work.

Rule 4: Always know your exit. Before entering a leveraged position, know how you exit it and what the exit costs. A forced exit at the worst time (which is when forced exits happen) should not be a financial catastrophe. Know your exit before you enter.

Rule 5: The cost of leverage is always higher than the stated rate. Interest costs are only part of the cost of leverage. There are administrative costs, compliance costs, the psychological cost of managing leveraged positions through volatility, and the opportunity cost of capital tied up in margin requirements. Honest accounting of the full cost of leverage often makes highly leveraged positions less attractive than they first appear.

Stress-Testing Before the Market Does It for You

Every leveraged position should be stress-tested before it is entered and periodically during its life. Stress testing means asking: what happens to this position under adverse scenarios? And specifically: what is the maximum loss I can sustain, and what happens if I sustain it?

Build a simple stress test for any significant leveraged position. Define three scenarios: base case (your expected outcome), adverse case (a bad but plausible outcome), and severe case (a crisis outcome). Calculate your financial position under each. If the severe case destroys your operation, the position is too large or too leveraged. Resize until the severe case, though painful, leaves you intact.

The psychological dimension of leverage deserves acknowledgment. Leverage is emotionally demanding. A 10% decline in an unleveraged position is uncomfortable. A 10% decline in a 5:1 leveraged position is a 50% loss of your equity, and it often happens faster than your nervous system can process. Operators who enter leveraged positions without having honestly considered and emotionally rehearsed the adverse scenarios tend to panic-sell at the worst times crystallizing losses that would have been recoverable if the position had been sized correctly and held with discipline.

LEVERAGE IS FORCE MULTIPLICATION - KNOW WHAT YOU ARE MULTIPLYING

Leverage multiplies outcomes. If you are right, it multiplies your gains. If you are wrong, it multiplies your losses. Before using leverage, be very clear about how confident you are in the underlying thesis, how much you would lose if you are completely wrong, and whether that loss is survivable. Leverage applied to a sound, well-researched position accelerates wealth. Leverage applied to speculation is gambling with borrowed money. The Operator knows the difference and acts accordingly.

The Operator who masters leverage understanding its mechanics, applying it with discipline, sizing it conservatively, and stress-testing positions before the market does it has access to the most powerful wealth-building tool in existence. The Operator who uses leverage recklessly has access to the most efficient wealth-destruction tool in existence. The difference is not the tool. It is the operator.

PART THREE:

The Operators Who Changed the Game

Chapter 10

Case Studies in Financial Domination: Lessons from the Masters

"The best investment you can make is in yourself. The more you learn, the more you earn." **Warren Buffett**

There is a temptation, in financial education, to treat the great investors and operators of history as almost supernatural beings blessed with gifts of intelligence, insight, or luck that place them fundamentally outside the reach of ordinary people. This is a comforting narrative for those who would rather admire from the sidelines than do the work. It is also wrong.

The Operators who built extraordinary wealth were not magical. They were systematic. They had frameworks ways of thinking about markets, risk, and capital that were more rigorous, more disciplined, and more honest than those of the people they outperformed. Their advantages were behavioral and analytical, not supernatural. And those advantages can be studied, understood, and at least partially replicated not to guarantee their specific results, but to build the same quality of thinking that made their results possible.

Warren Buffett: The System behind the Legend

Everyone knows Warren Buffett. Most people think they know what he does: buy good stocks and hold them forever. This is the surface-level narrative that has become so simplified as to be nearly useless as a practical framework.

The actual Buffett system particularly in his early career at the Buffett Partnership, Ltd. in the 1950s and 1960s was far more sophisticated and far more aggressive than the "patient long-term investor" mythology suggests. Buffett in his early years was a student and practitioner of Benjamin Graham's "cigar butt" investing: finding deeply undervalued companies often ugly, unfashionable businesses with assets worth far more than their market price and buying them cheaply enough that even mediocre outcomes would produce acceptable returns. He called these investments "cigar butts" because they had one good puff left in them even if they were otherwise undesirable.

He also ran what he called "special situations" arbitrage investments in companies involved in mergers, liquidations, and corporate restructurings where the mathematical outcome of the event was more predictable than the direction of general market prices. These were not passive, long-term holds. They were active, event-driven investments requiring continuous research and sharp analysis of probabilities and payoffs.

The Buffett Partnership generated compound annual returns of approximately 29.5% over its thirteen-year existence, against the Dow Jones Industrial Average's approximately 7.4% annualized over the same period. This is not the performance of a buy-and-hold investor in great businesses. It is the performance of a supremely rigorous value investor exploiting mispricing with the full intellectual force of a financial system built by his mentor, Graham.

As Buffett's capital grew to a scale where small, obscure value opportunities could no longer move the needle, his approach evolved influenced significantly by his partner Charlie Munger toward what he describes as buying "wonderful companies at fair prices." This is the familiar Berkshire Hathaway model: companies with durable competitive advantages ("moats"), strong management, and the ability to compound capital at high rates over long periods.

The Operator lessons from Buffett's approach at every stage:

- Understand your edge completely. Buffett didn't invest in what he found interesting. He invested in what he understood deeply enough to have a genuine analytical advantage. His "circle of competence" was precise and honestly bounded.
- Patience is a competitive advantage. In markets dominated by short-term thinking, the investor with a genuine long-term orientation who can hold through volatility and ignore noise has a structural edge over shorter-term competitors.
- Price matters even for quality. No business is so wonderful that any price is justified. The margin of safety buying below intrinsic value was central to Buffett's thinking at every stage of his career.
- The power of float. Berkshire's insurance operations generate float premiums received before claims are paid that Buffett invests essentially as free leverage. Understanding the business model behind the investment is as important as understanding the investment itself.

Ray Dalio: Principles, Systems, and the All-Weather Machine

Ray Dalio founded Bridgewater Associates in 1975 from his New York City apartment. By the time he stepped back from day-to-day management decades later, it had grown to become the world's largest hedge fund, managing over $100 billion in assets. The story of Bridgewater's growth is inseparable from the intellectual framework Dalio built and relentlessly refined over decades.

The core of Dalio's investment philosophy is the concept of "radical transparency" applied to markets: the attempt to understand economic and market reality with complete honesty, stripped of wishful thinking, narrative bias, and comfortable assumptions. This meant building what Dalio calls a "machine" a systematic, algorithmic process for identifying economic conditions and positioning assets accordingly rather than relying on individual judgment and intuition that are inevitably subject to psychological distortion.

Dalio's most widely discussed investment framework is the all-weather portfolio concept introduced in the previous chapter built on the recognition that different asset classes perform differently across the four combinations of rising/falling growth and rising/falling inflation. By balancing a portfolio across these environments rather than betting on a single economic outcome, Dalio aimed to create a portfolio that would perform adequately in any environment rather than superbly in some and catastrophically in others.

The other intellectual contribution for which Dalio is known particularly since the publication of his book *Principles* is the explicit codification of decision-making frameworks. Rather than relying on intuition or individual judgment, Dalio built systems: explicit, written principles for how to think about specific categories of decisions, which could then be applied consistently and evaluated objectively against outcomes. The aspiration was to identify cognitive biases and eliminate them from decision-making through systematic process.

The Operator lessons from Dalio:

- Systems beat intuition in complex, data-rich environments. Build explicit decision frameworks and apply them consistently rather than making each decision anew from scratch.

- Radical honesty about your own errors and biases is a competitive advantage, not a character flaw. The investor who can accurately assess what they got wrong and why learns faster than the one who rationalizes poor outcomes.
- Economic cycles are legible if you study them. Dalio's "debt cycle" framework the analysis of how leverage builds, peaks, and unwinds across economies is a powerful macro analytical tool available to any investor who studies it seriously.

Jesse Livermore: The Lessons of the Greatest Speculator

Jesse Livermore is a more complicated case study than Buffett or Dalio, not a model to emulate wholesale, but a source of lessons both positive and cautionary that illuminates the psychology of markets in ways that are permanently useful.

Livermore was the greatest stock market speculator of the early twentieth century. In 1929, he shorted the market ahead of the catastrophic crash and reportedly profited $100 million - equivalent to over $1.7 billion in today's money - in a single year. He had also been broke multiple times before and would be broke again. His story is the story of extraordinary analytical intelligence married to insufficient emotional discipline, and his life ended in tragedy.

What Livermore understood about markets that most of his contemporaries didn't was the importance of reading the "tape" the real-time flow of price and volume information as a signal about institutional and market behavior rather than as a number to be rationalized by fundamental analysis. He was one of the first to articulate what later became technical analysis: the idea that price patterns reflect the aggregate behavior of market participants and can be read as indicators of future price direction.

His understanding of market psychology that markets move on sentiment, fear, and greed as much as on fundamental value was a generation ahead of academic finance. He articulated the concept of staying in strong trends until they reverse rather than selling too early or averaging down into losing positions principles that remain foundational to trend-following and momentum investing approaches today.

The cautionary lesson of Livermore is equally powerful: intelligence and insight without discipline, risk management, and emotional control produce extreme volatility in outcomes spectacular highs and catastrophic lows. Livermore repeatedly made fortunes and lost them because he broke his own rules, added to losing positions, abandoned the discipline that produced his wins, and allowed psychological states of overconfidence and desperation to override systematic thinking.

The Operator lesson: the same intelligence that identifies opportunity will destroy you if it isn't paired with the discipline to manage risk and the honesty to know when you are operating outside your principles.

What They Had in Common

Despite operating in different eras, with different strategies and different asset classes, Buffett, Dalio, and Livermore and the roster of other great financial operators share a set of characteristics that transcend their specific methods:

Systems thinking: Each built a framework for thinking about markets that was more explicit and disciplined than the random intuition most investors rely on. The framework created consistency; consistency created compounding.

Asymmetric bets: Each was willing to make large, concentrated bets when the evidence was compelling and the risk-reward asymmetry was strongly favorable and hold smaller, more diversified positions when the evidence was less clear. They did not "diversify" for the sake of diversification when they had genuine conviction.

Emotional discipline: The great operators controlled their emotions rather than being controlled by them particularly during extreme market conditions when the crowd's behavior most strongly diverged from rational analysis. This is perhaps the most consistently identified characteristic of superior long-term investment performance.

Continuous learning: None of the great operators ever stopped studying. Markets change, economies evolve, and the investor who relies on yesterday's framework without continuous updating eventually becomes a cautionary tale rather than a success story.

OPERATOR STUDY METHOD

Don't read the biographies of great investors looking for their specific trades to copy. Read them looking for their decision frameworks — the underlying principles they applied to generate those trades. The specific trades belong to their specific market conditions. The frameworks can be adapted and applied in any era.

Chapter 11

The Operator Who Failed - And What It Cost

"Success is a lousy teacher. It seduces smart people into thinking they can't lose." **Bill Gates**

The study of failure is at least as valuable as the study of success, and possibly more so. Success is confounded by luck; sometimes people succeed for the wrong reasons and the success masks the flaws that will eventually catch up with them. Failure is cleaner. The structural errors that produce catastrophic outcomes are usually identifiable in retrospect, and they tend to be recurring errors the same fundamental mistakes appearing in different costumes across different markets, different eras, and different industries.

The Operator studies failure not to be paralyzed by the possibility of it, but to build defenses against the specific failure modes that have proven most lethal to financial operations. These are the modes we examine in this chapter.

Long-Term Capital Management: When Genius Was Not Enough

Long-Term Capital Management (LTCM) was founded in 1994 by John Meriwether, formerly of Salomon Brothers, and its board included two Nobel Prize-winning economists, Myron Scholes and Robert Merton, whose work on options pricing had transformed the field of quantitative finance. The fund raised $1.25 billion at inception the largest hedge fund launch in history to that point and generated extraordinary returns of 21%, 43%, and 41% in its first three years.

LTCM's strategy was built on the mathematical principle of mean reversion: the idea that prices of related securities that had diverged from their historical relationships would eventually converge back to those relationships. The fund would identify these divergences between on-the-run and off-the-run Treasury bonds, between mortgage-backed securities and comparable Treasuries, between equity volatility implied by options and realized volatility and take positions that would profit when the spreads converged. These were essentially statistical arbitrage positions, backed by the sophisticated quantitative models of some of the most intellectually formidable people in finance.

The fatal structural flaw was not in the models themselves, which identified real statistical relationships. The flaw was in the leverage: LTCM employed leverage ratios of approximately 25-to-1, meaning that for every $1 of its own capital, it controlled approximately $25 of assets. At its peak, the fund had $4.7 billion in equity capital but held positions worth $125 billion. By some estimates, its notional exposure to derivatives was over $1 trillion.

In 1998, the Russian government defaulted on its domestic debt and devalued the ruble. This triggered a global flight to safety investors around the world sold anything perceived as risky and bought US Treasury bonds. The spreads that LTCM had bet would converge didn't converge. They widened dramatically, because in a crisis, statistical relationships that hold over long periods can violate badly over short periods when fear drives all market participants to the same safe haven simultaneously. Every position in LTCM's portfolio moved against it simultaneously the exact scenario that its risk models had assigned an astronomically low probability.

As the positions deteriorated, LTCM faced margin calls demands from creditors that it post additional collateral or reduce positions. To meet margin calls, it had to sell positions into falling markets, which further depressed prices and triggered further margin calls. This is the margin spiral that leveraged investors have faced in every crisis in history. By September 1998, LTCM had lost $4.6 billion nearly its entire equity capital in fewer than four months.

The Federal Reserve Bank of New York, alarmed by the potential for LTCM's forced liquidation to destabilize the broader financial system, orchestrated a bailout by a consortium of fourteen major banks, which collectively injected $3.625 billion of capital in exchange for 90% of the fund's equity. The fund was gradually wound down over the following two years.

The lessons for every Operator who ever picks up a leveraged position are permanent and non-negotiable:

- Statistical models describe historical behavior in normal markets. They do not adequately capture the behavior of markets during crises, when fear, forced selling, and liquidity collapse create correlations and movements that the historical data never observed.
- Leverage that is sustainable in normal conditions can become fatal during brief periods of extreme market stress. The critical question is not "does this leverage

work in normal conditions?" but "what happens to this leverage in the worst three weeks of the worst year in recent history?"

- Intellectual confidence does not protect against structural risk. LTCM employed some of the most mathematically sophisticated people in finance. Their models were elegant and their reasoning was internally consistent. None of this mattered when the market moved against them with 25:1 leverage and no exits.
- Liquidity risk is the risk that kills leveraged operations. LTCM had positions that, under normal conditions, were liquid and tradable. Under crisis conditions, they became illiquid no one would buy what LTCM needed to sell. Leverage applied to illiquid assets is among the most dangerous combinations in finance.

Enron: When the Structure Becomes the Fraud

The story of Enron Corporation which was the seventh-largest company in the United States by revenue in 2001 and bankrupt by December of the same year is primarily a story about the corruption of financial structures and the catastrophic consequences of building a company on concealment rather than value creation.

Enron began as a conventional natural gas pipeline company after the merger of Houston Natural Gas and InterNorth in 1985. Under CEO Jeffrey Skilling, it transformed itself or rather; it positioned itself publicly as a revolutionary financial and trading company, using sophisticated financial engineering to transform the energy business. In reality, Enron's financial engineering was increasingly devoted to concealing the reality of a business that was not generating the returns it reported.

Enron used a network of off-balance-sheet entities special purpose vehicles with opaque structures to move debt and underperforming assets off its financial statements, making its balance sheet appear stronger than it was. It used mark-to-market accounting valuing assets and contracts at their theoretical long-term market value rather than their current realizable value to book future profits immediately, creating the appearance of earnings from contracts that might not produce those earnings for years, if at all. It relied on increasingly complex transactions with related parties to manufacture revenue and obscure losses.

The fraud worked, for a time, because the complexity itself was a defense mechanism. Analysts and investors who didn't fully understand the financial statements assumed the complexity reflected sophistication rather than concealment. The culture of Enron - aggressive, status-driven, and deeply contemptuous of any questioning discouraged internal challenge. Auditors, bankers, lawyers, and rating agencies who had financial interests in Enron's continued success found reasons not to look too closely.

When the edifice began to crack a Fortune magazine article in March 2001 raised questions about Enron's earnings quality, and mounting questions about the off-balance-sheet entities began circulating the collapse was swift. Investors who had believed Enron was a technology company trading at a premium valuation discovered they had been holding a highly leveraged, cash-burning entity whose reported profits were largely illusory. The stock, which had traded as high as $90 per share in 2000, was trading at less than $1 by November 2001.

The Operator lessons from Enron are about the ethics of financial structures, not just their mechanics:

- Any business or investment structure whose primary function is concealment rather than value creation is a fraud waiting to be discovered. The structures may be technically legal Enron's lawyers were very skilled at operating near the legal line but they are not sustainable.

- Complexity that cannot be explained is a red flag, not a sign of sophistication. If you cannot understand what a business or financial structure is doing and why, in plain language, the complexity may exist to hide something you need to know.
- Culture that punishes questioning is a structural vulnerability. Operations businesses, investment funds, financial structures that suppress honest internal feedback are deprived of the self-correcting mechanism that allows problems to be identified and fixed before they become catastrophic.

The 2008 Real Estate Collapse: The Danger of Over-levered Operators

The 2007-2008 financial crises produced thousands of individual stories of real estate operators who had built what appeared to be impressive operations portfolios of investment properties, development projects, and commercial real estate on leverage that proved unsustainable when the credit cycle turned.

The structural errors were consistent across these operators regardless of their sophistication:

Over-reliance on short-term financing for long-term assets: Many real estate operators funded the acquisition and development of properties that would take years to produce their full value using short-term bridge loans and revolving credit facilities that required frequent renewal. When the credit markets froze in 2008, these loans could not be renewed, and operators were forced to sell assets into the worst possible market conditions.

Absence of cash flow cushions: In the boom years preceding 2008, real estate operators routinely financed properties at leverage ratios that left little or no margin for error the property's rental income, under optimistic occupancy assumptions, just barely serviced the debt. When occupancy fell or rents declined, cash flow turned negative, and the operator had no reserves to absorb the shortfall. Missed payments triggered default provisions, which triggered forced sales.

Concentration in a single geography and asset type: Operators who had built portfolios of single-family homes in Phoenix, Vegas, or South Florida on markets that had experienced the most extreme price appreciation and correspondingly suffered the most extreme price declines discovered that geographic concentration amplified losses in exactly the scenarios where diversification would have provided the most protection.

Over-reliance on appreciation rather than cash flow: The investor who buys a property expecting to sell it quickly at a higher price with no ability to sustain the holding if the sale doesn't happen on schedule is not an investor. They are a speculator. Speculators are dependent on timing that markets do not guarantee. Operators build for cash flow and let appreciation be the bonus, not the plan.

The Operator's Checklist for Avoiding Catastrophic Failure

Failure Mode	Warning Sign	Operator Defense

Failure Mode	Warning Sign	Operator Defense
Excessive leverage	Positions sized at maximum possible leverage	Use conservative leverage; stress test at 2x adverse scenario
Short-term financing of long-term assets	Loans expiring within 2 years on long-term holds	Match debt duration to asset duration; always
Complexity as concealment	Structures you can't explain in plain language	If you can't explain it, don't do it

Failure Mode	Warning Sign	Operator Defense
Model risk	Returns dependent on historical correlations holding	Test strategy against historical crises, not just normal periods
No cash flow cushion	Debt barely serviceable at optimistic assumptions	Underwrite to break-even at 75-80% of optimistic revenue
Geographic/sector concentration	More than 50% of portfolio in single market	Deliberate diversification; monitor concentration risk quarterly

Failure Mode	Warning Sign	Operator Defense
Culture of yes	No one in your circle challenges your assumptions	Actively seek critical analysis; reward honest dissent

The Operator who studies failure does not become timid. They become precise. Every failure examined is a defense built. Every structural error identified in someone else's operation is a guardrail installed in your own. Failure at scale tends to come not from one catastrophic decision but from a cascade of smaller decisions that each seemed reasonable in isolation each one adding a small increment of fragility until the structure can no longer bear the load. The Operator's job is to see the fragility accumulating before it reaches the breaking point.

Chapter 12

The New Operators: How the Digital Age Changed the Battlefield

"The internet is a level playing field only if you're willing to do the work to make it one." **The Operator's Creed**

The financial world that existed twenty years ago and the financial world that exists today are different in ways that matter enormously for the individual Operator. Not in the underlying principles — human psychology, risk and return, the power of compounding, the danger of leverage — those are permanent. But in the specific tools, the information landscape, the accessible asset classes, and the nature of institutional competitive advantage.

The digital revolution has simultaneously created new opportunities for the Operator and new categories of danger. Understanding both is essential.

Fintech Disruption: Democratizing the Institutional Toolkit

The financial technology revolution of the past decade has made tools previously available only to institutional investors accessible to individual operators at dramatically reduced cost. This democratization is real, meaningful, and ongoing.

Commission-free trading, whatever its complexities around payment for order flow (discussed in Chapter 2), has eliminated the friction cost that previously made frequent portfolio rebalancing or small-scale investing economically irrational. Fractional share investing is the ability to buy $50 worth of Amazon or $100 of Berkshire Hathaway regardless of the full share price and removes the barrier of high per-share prices from individual stock investing. Automated robo-advisors provide sophisticated, low-cost portfolio management based on Nobel Prize-winning academic research in asset allocation for fees that are a fraction of what a traditional advisor would charge for significantly less sophisticated service.

Access to alternative assets has been dramatically democratized. Platforms like Fundrise, RealtyMogul, and Arrived allow accredited and, in some cases, nonaccredited investors to participate in commercial and residential real estate investments with minimums that would have been laughably small in the institutional context. Platforms like Republic, AngelList, and various crowdfunding platforms allow participation in venture capital and startup investing at minimums far below traditional VC fund thresholds. Private credit platforms allow individual investors to participate in direct lending to small businesses.

Information access has been transformed. Financial data that required expensive Bloomberg terminals or direct institutional subscriptions is now broadly available through platforms like Yahoo Finance, FRED (the Federal Reserve's data platform), Quandl, and dozens of others. Earnings calls, regulatory filings, and corporate disclosures that once required specialized services to access and organize are now available instantly and for free through EDGAR, company investor relations websites, and aggregator platforms. This information democratization has real implications for the nature of individual investor competitive advantage.

Algorithmic Trading and Robo-Advisors: When to Use Them and When Not To

Algorithmic trading - trading executed by computer programs based on pre-defined rules - dominates modern financial markets. Estimates suggest that algorithmic and high-frequency trading accounts for 60-70% of all US equity trading volume. This is the environment in which every individual investor's trades are executed, and understanding it shapes how you should approach trading.

For most Operators, the practical implication of algorithmic dominance in markets is: don't try to beat algorithms at the high-frequency game. The speed, data access, and computational resources that institutional algorithmic traders have are not replicable by an individual. Any strategy that depends on speed of execution, minute-to-minute price patterns, or very short-term technical signals is playing in territory where the institutional players have overwhelming advantages.

What algorithms are less good at: long-term fundamental analysis, qualitative assessment of business quality and management, synthesis of non-quantitative information, and patient positioning for multi-year outcomes. These are areas where human judgment, applied carefully, can still provide genuine edge - and they are precisely the areas where the individual Operator can compete effectively.

Robo-advisors - automated investment platforms that build and manage diversified portfolios based on your risk tolerance, time horizon, and financial goals - are genuinely useful tools for Operators who want passive, systematic portfolio management at low cost without the complexity of direct management. They excel at tax-loss harvesting, automatic rebalancing, and broad asset class diversification. What they cannot do: qualitative assessment of specific investment opportunities, tactical allocation based on macro views, alternative asset management, or anything requiring human judgment about specific circumstances. Think of a robo-advisor as a reliable automatic pilot for the passive portion of your portfolio, not as a replacement for strategic thinking about your overall financial architecture.

Blockchain, Tokenized Assets, and Decentralized Finance: The Honest Assessment

No honest treatment of the digital age's impact on financial markets can ignore the rise of blockchain technology, cryptocurrencies, and the broader ecosystem of decentralized finance (DeFi). And no honest treatment of these topics can avoid acknowledging that they are simultaneously genuinely interesting and extraordinarily prone to speculation, fraud, and catastrophically poor outcomes for unprepared participants.

The technology itself distributed ledger technology, smart contracts; cryptographic security is real and has genuine applications. The ability to create programmable money, to automate complex financial agreements through smart contracts, and to build financial infrastructure that operates without the intermediaries who currently extract fees from every financial transaction these are meaningful innovations with significant long-term potential.

Bitcoin, the original and most widely adopted cryptocurrency, has proven its resilience as a network and its ability to store value over its approximately fifteen-year history. Whether it represents a superior store of value to gold, whether it will be adopted as a global reserve currency alternative, or whether it will ultimately be supplanted by a central bank digital currency these remain genuinely open questions. What is clear is that Bitcoin has generated extraordinary returns from its early price levels, has also experienced drawdowns of 75-85% multiple times, and is not a riskless or even moderate-risk asset. The

Operator who holds a small allocation 1-5% of portfolio with full acceptance that it may go to zero treats it as what it most honestly is: an asymmetric bet on a genuinely novel technology whose future adoption is uncertain but whose upside in success scenarios is very large.

The broader crypto ecosystem - the thousands of altcoins, the various DeFi protocols, the NFT market, and the various "Web3" applications - has been marked by extraordinary speculation, fraud, and the destruction of capital on a massive scale. Dozens of major crypto projects, exchanges, and funds that were worth billions of dollars on paper have gone to zero, taking their investors with them. The lack of regulatory oversight, the complexity of the technology, and the marketing effectiveness of projects that were substantively worthless have made the broader crypto space a killing field for underprepared retail investors.

The Operator's approach to blockchain and crypto: distinguish the technology from the speculation. Small, considered exposure to Bitcoin or Ethereum (the two most established projects with the longest track records) in the context of a diversified portfolio sized so that a complete loss would not be catastrophic is a defensible position. Active trading of altcoins, participation in unaudited DeFi protocols, or large concentration in any crypto asset is speculation, not investment, and should be treated as such.

Tokenized assets - the use of blockchain to represent ownership of real-world assets like real estate, private equity, or commodities are a genuinely interesting development that may significantly change access to alternative investments over the coming decade. The technology for fractional ownership of previously illiquid assets is real and the potential to democratize access to institutional-quality investments is meaningful. The current state of the market for most tokenized assets is still early, regulatory frameworks are uncertain, and liquidity is generally poor. This is a space to monitor and understand, not one to rush into ahead of regulatory clarity and market maturity.

Information Asymmetry in the Digital Age

Here is the paradox of the information revolution in financial markets: more information is available to more people than ever before, yet information asymmetry still exists and may in some ways have increased rather than decreased.

The reason is signal-to-noise. The digital age has not just increased the supply of information it has overwhelmingly increased the supply of noise. Misinformation, partial information, agenda-driven analysis, social media speculation, and the constant churn of financial content designed to generate clicks rather than insight has created a world in which the investor who can distinguish reliable signal from noise is at a greater advantage than ever.

True information edges in modern markets are more specific than ever. They come from: deep expertise in a specific industry or geography that allows superior qualitative assessment of business quality; primary research involving direct conversation with customers, competitors, and suppliers rather than secondary analysis of public information; disciplined, systematic processing of data that most investors consume but don't organize into actionable frameworks; and behavioral advantages - the ability to maintain a rational long-term perspective when the social and emotional pressures of the market are pulling strongly in the opposite direction.

The Operator who builds genuine domain expertise in a specific industry, geographic market, or asset class has an information advantage in that domain that is real and durable. Breadth of attention without depth of expertise produces noise consumption, not insight. The Operator chooses depth.

THE DIGITAL AGE OPERATOR'S EDGE

In a world where everyone has access to the same financial headlines, the Operator's edge comes from:

1. ***Better analytical frameworks for interpreting information everyone can see.***
2. ***Deeper expertise in specific domains that produces better qualitative judgment.***
3. ***Better behavioral discipline the ability to act on analysis rather than emotion.***
4. ***Strategic use of digital tools to reduce costs and improve execution. The edge is not in the information. It is in the thinking that the information informs.***

The digital age has made the Operator's toolkit richer, cheaper, and more accessible than at any prior point in history. It has also made the noise louder, the distractions more seductive, and the potential for self-destructive speculative behavior more available. The digital tools serve the Operator who brings discipline, framework, and genuine expertise to them. They punish the participant who treats them as shortcuts to wealth without the underlying foundation.

PART FOUR:

Building Your Operation for World Domination

Chapter 13

Designing Your Personal Financial Command Center

"An organization, no matter how well designed, is only as good as the people who live and work in it." Dee Hock

---

An Operator doesn't just react to their financial life. An Operator designs it. The difference between a financial life that is managed one that responds to events, pays bills when they arrive, invests when they get around to it, and makes financial decisions one at a time without strategic context and a financial life that is commanded one that operates according to a deliberate architecture, with clear systems, precise monitoring, and a professional team providing expert support is the difference between playing checkers and playing chess.

This chapter is about building the command center. Not in a complex or costly way, simplicity is a feature, not a concession but deliberately, with each component chosen for a specific function and integrated into a system that runs your finances with minimal friction and maximum strategic effectiveness.

Building Your Operator Stack: Brokerage, Bank, Credit, and Entity Structure

Every Operator needs a financial stack - the set of accounts, institutions, and entities through which their money flows. Most people have a financial stack by default: whatever bank their parents used, whatever brokerage their company 401(k) is held at, the credit cards they signed up for because of airline miles. An Operator builds their stack deliberately, with each component selected for specific capabilities.

Banking: Your banking relationship is the foundation. You need a primary operating account for day-to-day transactions and a high-yield savings account for your cash reserves (your emergency fund and near-term capital deployment fund). For the operating account, a national bank with good digital banking infrastructure is fine. For the high-yield savings, an online bank or money market fund typically offers meaningfully better rates than traditional banks, particularly in higher-rate environments. As your operation grows, a relationship with a private bank or wealth management division of a major institution can provide access to better loan terms, investment products, and professional services the threshold for these relationships varies but typically begins at $250,000-500,000 in liquid assets.

Brokerage: Your brokerage is where your investment portfolio lives. For most Operators, one primary brokerage account is sufficient, supplemented by tax-advantaged accounts (IRAs, 401(k)). Evaluate brokerage platforms on: investment selection (can you access all the asset classes and funds you want?), execution quality (how good is order routing?), research and tools (does the platform support the analysis you do?), and service quality (can you get a human on the phone when you need one?). Tax-advantaged accounts Roth IRA, Traditional IRA, SEP-IRA, Solo 401(k) should be maximized before taxable accounts for most Operators, given the extraordinary compounding benefit of tax-free or tax-deferred growth.

Credit: Credit is a tool, not a score to protect for its own sake. Build excellent credit consistently paying on time, maintaining low utilization relative to limits, building a long history because good credit is the foundation for accessing leverage when you want it at the best available terms. As your operation grows, you want access to business credit lines, investment property financing, and potentially SBA loans or other business financing tools. These require excellent credit established well in advance of when you need them. The Operator who begins building credit infrastructure before it's needed has access to financing when opportunities arise; the one who builds it reactively often misses the opportunity window.

Entity structure: How you hold assets personally, through an LLC, through a trust, through a corporation has significant tax and legal implications. The default (holding everything personally) is the worst structure from both a tax and asset protection perspective. A proper entity structure, designed with your CPA and attorney, separates your personal assets from your business and investment activities, provides liability protection, enables tax optimization strategies, and creates the foundation for estate planning. We'll go deeper on specific entity structures in Chapter 15.

The Dashboard: Tracking Net Worth, Cash Flow, and Exposure

You cannot manage what you do not measure. The Operator maintains a financial dashboard that provides a clear, current picture of their financial position at all times.

This does not require expensive software a well-designed spreadsheet, updated monthly, is sufficient for most Operators. What matters is the consistency and completeness of the data.

The Operator's dashboard has four components:

Net worth statement: Assets minus liabilities, categorized by type. Liquid assets (cash, publicly traded securities), real estate (estimated market value minus mortgage balances), business equity (estimated value of business interests minus business liabilities), retirement accounts, and other assets. Updated monthly. The net worth statement answers the fundamental question: where are you now, and is the number moving in the right direction?

Cash flow statement: All income sources and all expenses, on a monthly basis. Not just a budget but an actual tracking of what flows in and what flows out. Income should be categorized by source: earned income (wages, self-employment), passive income (rental income, royalties, dividends), and portfolio income (capital gains, interest). Expenses should be categorized enough to identify where money is going without excessive granularity. The cash flow statement answers: are you generating surplus capital for deployment, and where is the money going?

Investment exposure summary: A concise view of your investment portfolio by asset class and geography. What percentage is in equities (domestic vs. international, large vs. small vs. emerging)? What percentage in real estate? Fixed income? Alternatives? What is the largest concentration risk the single position or sector that, if it went wrong, would hurt most? The exposure summary answers: are you positioned where you intend to be, and where are your concentrations?

Liability and debt schedule: Every debt, organized by balance, interest rate, maturity, and monthly payment. This is not just for information it informs debt payoff strategy (higher-rate debt is generally prioritized for payoff, but Operator-level debt management also considers tax deductibility and the opportunity cost of capital used for paydown versus investment). The liability schedule answers: what are the obligations that must be met regardless of investment performance?

Review your dashboard monthly. Have a more comprehensive quarterly review that includes year-to-date progress toward annual goals and an assessment of whether your asset allocation has drifted from your target. Have an annual comprehensive review that reassesses goals, adjusts strategies, and plans for the coming year with your financial team.

Automation and systems that run your finances without constant attention

The behavioral finance research on this point is unambiguous: automated financial systems produce better outcomes than willpower-dependent ones. When saving, investing, and debt repayment happen automatically when the money moves before you can decide to spend it, the results are consistently superior to systems that require active decision-making at each step.

The Operator automates ruthlessly:

Automate savings and investment contributions: Set up automatic transfers to your investment accounts, retirement accounts, and savings accounts on payday. The amount you invest should be the first decision you make, not the last one after expenses are paid. Pay yourself first is not a cliché it is the mechanism by which most successful wealth-building actually happens.

Automate bill payment: Every fixed expense rent or mortgage, utilities, insurance, loan payments should be on autopay. This eliminates late payment risk, removes unnecessary friction from your monthly routine, and frees cognitive capacity for decisions that actually require your attention.

Automate rebalancing: Most modern investment platforms offer automatic rebalancing the system automatically sells overweight positions and buys underweight ones to maintain your target allocation. This enforces buy-low-sell-high discipline mechanically, removing the emotional challenge of deliberately selling what has gone up and buying what has gone down.

Automate tax-loss harvesting: Robo-advisors and some premium investment platforms offer automated tax-loss harvesting. For taxable investment accounts, this can add meaningful after-tax return over time with zero additional effort.

Hiring Your Financial Team

The Operator does not try to do everything alone. At every level of wealth, there are professional services that generate returns far exceeding their cost and the earlier you invest in the right professional relationships, the more value they create over time.

Accountant/CPA: Not a tax preparer that fills out forms based on the information you give them a strategic tax advisor who understands your business, investment portfolio, and financial goals and proactively designs your tax structure. Interview at least three CPAs before selecting one. Ask specifically about their experience with clients in your income range and investment profile. Ask for examples of proactive tax planning they've done for clients not just tax return preparation, but strategies they identified and implemented. Fee range varies widely, but expects $2,000-$10,000 per year for comprehensive tax strategy and preparation at early-to-mid Operator levels.

Attorney: You need two types of attorney: a business/corporate attorney for entity formation, contracts, and business transactions, and an estate planning attorney for wills, trusts, and beneficiary designations. A third type a tax attorney becomes important at higher wealth levels for complex tax planning and any tax controversy. These are not relationships you invoke only when crisis arrives. They are relationships you build in advance, so you have a trusted advisor when decisions need to be made under time pressure.

Financial planner/advisor: Be deliberate about the fee structure. A fee-only fiduciary financial advisor one who charges you directly for their services (flat fee, hourly, or a percentage of assets managed) and is legally required to act in your best interest is a very different relationship from a commission-based advisor who earns money when you buy the products they recommend. Both exist. Know which one you're dealing with.

Vet every professional rigorously. Check credentials. Check disciplinary histories (FINRA's BrokerCheck for financial advisors, the state bar for attorneys). Ask for references. Talk to their other clients if possible. And above all maintain your own understanding of your financial situation. Your advisors work for you. That relationship only functions correctly if you are informed enough to evaluate what they're telling you.

THE COMMAND CENTER PRINCIPLE

Your financial command center is not a place. It is a system — of accounts, data, automation, and professional relationships — that gives you complete situational awareness of your financial operation and the professional support to make every major decision with expert input. Building this system is not a one-time event. It is a continuous process of refinement as your operation grows, your needs evolve, and better tools and professionals become available.

Chapter 14

The Operator's Income Architecture

"The goal is not to work for money. The goal is to have money work for you." **Robert Kiyosaki**

The single greatest financial misconception carried by most working people is that income is a linear function of time. Work more hours, earn more money. Stop working, stop earning. Under this model, you are always one serious illness, one layoff, or one extended disability away from financial catastrophe. The Operator's income architecture is built on a fundamentally different model: income that flows from assets and systems rather than exclusively from your personal time.

This is not a dismissal of earned income. Earned income from your job, your business, your skills and expertise is almost certainly the most important building block in your early Operator career. It is the capital that funds the investment, the business equity that creates cash flow, the surplus that builds the passive income layer. But the architecture of the Operator's income structure is designed so that, over time, the ratio of active-to-passive income shifts consistently toward passive. This is what financial independence looks like in practice: not the elimination of work (most Operators keep working because they love what they do), but the elimination of the requirement to work as the price of financial survival.

Multiple Streams: Active, Passive, Portfolio, and Business Income

The IRS, in its own way, provides a useful taxonomy of income types that map closely to the Operator's framework. There are three basic categories: earned (active) income, passive income, and portfolio income. The Operator adds a fourth category business income that has distinct characteristics from pure employment income.

Active/earned income is what you generate through direct personal effort. Wages from employment. Fees from client work. Income from services you personally provide. This is the highest-taxed category subject to ordinary income rates plus payroll/self-employment taxes and the most time-dependent. Earned income is foundational in early career and should be maximized through skill development, positioning, and negotiation. But it is inherently capped by time and personal capacity.

Business income deserves separate treatment from simple earned income because a business once built can generate income that scales beyond the personal time of its founder. A business with employees, systems, and recurring customer relationships can generate cash flow that continues when you're on vacation, that grows without proportional growth in your personal effort, and that can eventually be sold for a multiple of its annual earnings, creating a capital event. Building a business even a small one is the most powerful active income strategy available to the individual Operator, precisely because it converts personal effort into a scalable, saleable asset.

Passive income is income generated from assets with minimal ongoing personal effort. Rental income from real estate, Royalties from intellectual property, Dividends and distributions from investments in businesses you don't actively manage, Interest income from lending, Limited partnership distributions. The defining characteristic of passive income is that it continues flowing even when you're not working which is exactly why it is the Operator's long-term target. Passive income also has specific tax treatment under IRS rules, including the passive activity loss rules that govern when passive losses can offset other income.

Portfolio income - capital gains, dividends from publicly traded securities, interest from bonds is the investment portfolio's contribution to your income stream. This category is particularly valuable because it is typically taxed at lower rates than earned income (qualified dividends and long-term capital gains at 15% or 20% for most Operators) and because a sufficiently large portfolio can generate portfolio income at a level that replaces earned income entirely the classic financial independence scenario.

Building for Income Replacement: The Freedom Number

The "Freedom Number" is simply the annual income required to cover your desired lifestyle expenses, provided entirely by passive and portfolio income. When your passive and portfolio income equals or exceeds your Freedom Number, employment becomes optional. You work because you choose to, not because you must.

Calculating your Freedom Number starts with an honest accounting of your lifestyle expenses not your current expenses, but the expenses of the lifestyle you actually want to live. Housing, food, transportation, healthcare, travel, entertainment, education for yourself and family, charitable giving and buffer for the unexpected. Add it up. That number, multiplied by 25 (which is the inverse of a 4% sustainable withdrawal rate from a portfolio a widely used retirement planning benchmark), gives you the portfolio size required to generate that income indefinitely through investment returns alone.

If your Freedom Number is $150,000 per year, your target portfolio at a 4% withdrawal rate is $3.75 million. If you have $50,000 per year in rental income, the portfolio needs to cover only $100,000, requiring $2.5 million in investments. Every dollar of passive income reduces the portfolio target by $25.

The practical implication: building passive income streams each of which incrementally reduces your portfolio requirement for financial freedom is one of the highest-leverage uses of your capital and effort during the accumulation phase. A rental property generating $10,000 per year in net income doesn't just produce $10,000 annually. It reduces your required portfolio by $250,000 the equivalent of adding $250,000 to your investment portfolio from a financial freedom perspective.

Cash Flow Assets vs. Appreciation Assets

The Operator's portfolio contains two broad categories of assets, with very different roles in the income architecture.

Cash flow assets generate regular income: rental properties with positive cash flow, dividend stocks, REITs, bonds, business interests with distributions, private credit investments. These assets produce current income they add to your passive income stream now, while you're building.

Appreciation assets build long-term wealth: growth stocks, development real estate, startup equity, a business in its growth phase. These assets may produce little or no current income but generate significant wealth through price appreciation over time which eventually becomes a capital event (a sale, a refinance) that funds additional cash flow assets.

The Operator needs both, in proportions appropriate to their phase and goals. Early in the accumulation phase, appreciation assets typically dominate you have time for growth to compound and less need for current income. As you approach financial independence, the balance shifts toward cash flow assets that can support your lifestyle without portfolio liquidation. In the distribution phase financial independence achieved cash flow assets carry the primary weight, supplemented by judicious appreciation asset sales.

Structuring for Both Short-Term Cash Flow and Long-Term Compounding

The eternal tension in income architecture is between extracting value today and compounding for tomorrow. Taking more current income from your investments reduces the capital that would otherwise compound. Reinvesting everything for growth means living below your financial potential in the near term. The Operator resolves this tension not through dogma "always reinvest everything" or "always maximize current income" but through deliberate design based on their specific situation.

A useful framework: segment your portfolio into buckets with different time horizons and different income/growth objectives. A near-term bucket (1-3 years of living expenses in very liquid, very stable assets) eliminates the need to sell long-term investments at inopportune times. A medium-term bucket (5-10 year time horizon, balanced between income and growth) generates the passive income stream that supplements earned income. A long-term bucket (10+ year horizon, growth-oriented, reinvesting all income) compounds aggressively for future wealth.

This bucket approach manages both the psychological challenge of market volatility (knowing your near-term living expenses are secured allows you to hold long-term positions through temporary market declines) and the structural challenge of matching cash flow timing to spending needs.

The Income Architecture Principle

Every investment decision an Operator makes should be evaluated in the context of the income architecture: Does this add to current cash flow? Does this compound long-term wealth? Does it fit the time horizon of the bucket it belongs in? A great investment placed in the wrong bucket a long-term appreciation play funded with money needed in two years is a structural error that undermines both the investment and the bucket system. Know the purpose of every dollar you deploy.

The Operator's income architecture is not built overnight. It is constructed over years, sometimes decades of deliberate investment in cash flow assets, business building, portfolio growth, and passive income accumulation. Each year, the architecture becomes more robust, the income streams more diverse, and the dependence on any single source reduced. That is the direction. Every month, the Operator moves further in that direction, and the compound effect of consistent movement over time creates outcomes that look, from the outside, like sudden success.

Chapter 15

Protecting the Operation: Legal and Financial Armor

"It's not enough to build wealth. You must defend it." **The Operator's Creed**

There is a pattern the Operator must recognize and avoid at all costs. A person works for years — building a business, accumulating real estate, growing an investment portfolio — and then loses a significant portion or all of it in a lawsuit, a creditor claim, a failed business that exposes personal assets, an inadequately planned estate that triggers unnecessary taxes and family conflict. The building was sound. The protection was absent. The outcome was catastrophic and preventable.

Asset protection is not a peripheral concern for the successful Operator. It is a core component of the financial architecture, built from the beginning and maintained continuously. The strategy costs relatively little when implemented properly and proactively. It can mean the difference between losing everything and surviving an adverse event intact.

LLCs, S-Corps, Trusts, and Holding Companies

The entity toolkit available to the American Operator is genuinely powerful when used correctly. Each entity type has specific characteristics; liability protection, tax treatment, operational flexibility that make it appropriate for specific purposes.

The Limited Liability Company (LLC) is the most versatile and widely used entity in the Operator's toolkit. It provides liability protection separating business liabilities from personal assets with relatively simple formation and maintenance requirements and flexible tax treatment (taxed as a sole proprietorship, partnership, S-corp, or C-corp depending on elections made). For real estate investors, a separate LLC for each investment property (or a small cluster of properties) is the standard asset protection approach: a lawsuit arising from one property is contained within that LLC's liability and cannot reach other properties held in separate entities or your personal assets.

The critical point about LLC liability protection: it only works if the LLC is properly maintained. This means separate bank accounts, no commingling of personal and business funds, proper documentation of business decisions, and adherence to the formalities of the entity's operating agreement. Courts can "pierce the corporate veil" ignore the LLC liability protection if the entity is found to have been operated as an alter ego of the individual owner, without genuine separation between personal and business activities. Maintaining that separation is not just good legal hygiene; it is the price of the protection the entity provides.

The S-Corporation, as discussed in Chapter 7, provides both liability protection and payroll tax savings for business owners who pay themselves a reasonable salary and take remaining profits as distributions not subject to self-employment tax. S-corps have restrictions limited to 100 shareholders, all of whom must be US citizens or residents, and only one class of stock that make them less flexible than LLCs for complex ownership structures, but for a single-owner or small-partner business, the tax advantages can be substantial.

Trusts serve multiple purposes in the Operator's asset protection and estate planning arsenal. A revocable living trust the most common trust avoids probate (the public, court-supervised process for distributing a deceased person's assets) and provides privacy, continuity of asset management if you become incapacitated, and simplified distribution of assets at death. It does not provide asset protection from creditors because you retain control over the trust and can revoke it.

Irrevocable trusts - trusts where you permanently transfer assets out of your name and give up control can provide significant asset protection because assets in an irrevocable trust are generally not reachable by your personal creditors. Various irrevocable trust structures serve specific purposes: Irrevocable Life Insurance Trusts (ILITs) hold life insurance outside your estate; Grantor Retained Annuity Trusts (GRATs) transfer appreciation on assets to heirs with minimal gift tax; Spousal Lifetime Access Trusts (SLATs) provide assets for a spouse while removing them from the estate. Each of these requires estate planning attorney guidance they are not DIY instruments.

Holding companies often a parent LLC or corporation that owns interests in subsidiary entities add another layer of organization and protection above individual operating entities. A holding company structure can provide additional liability separation between different lines of business or investment categories, estate planning flexibility, and centralized management of a complex operation. The complexity cost is higher more entities, more administration, more tax returns and the benefit only justifies the cost at meaningful scale, typically several significant operating units or real estate investments.

Asset Protection Strategies for the Operator's Wealth at Every Level

Asset protection strategy should be proportional to your wealth and your liability exposure not a one-size-fits-all prescription.

At the early accumulation phase (net worth below $500,000): the most important steps are maintaining separate business entities for any business activities, maximizing retirement accounts (which are generally protected from creditors under federal law), and ensuring adequate insurance coverage. The cost of sophisticated asset protection structures is not yet justified by the amount of wealth at risk.

At the mid-accumulation phase ($500,000 to $2 million): entity structures for each significant investment or business become important. A revocable living trust for estate planning is worth establishing. A liability umbrella insurance policy (discussed below) is essential. For high-liability professions (physicians, attorneys, contractors), more proactive asset protection planning is warranted regardless of wealth level.

At the established Operator level ($2 million and above): the full range of structures holding company architectures, irrevocable trusts, more sophisticated estate planning vehicles justifies the cost and complexity. An annual review with an estate planning attorney and CPA ensures the structure keeps pace with growing wealth and evolving estate planning laws.

Insurance: The Boring Tool That Saves Operations

Insurance is not an exciting topic. It generates no returns, creates no cash flow, and offers nothing but the promise of compensation if something goes terribly wrong. Yet the Operator who is adequately insured and the one who is not are in entirely different positions when the catastrophic event which comes for everyone eventually arrives.

The essential insurance coverage for every Operator:

Umbrella liability insurance is the single highest-value-per-dollar insurance policy most Operators don't have. An umbrella policy provides liability coverage above and beyond what your auto and homeowner's insurance provides typically in $1 million to $5 million increments for personal liability claims. Someone is injured on your property. You're in a serious car accident. A liability judgment is entered against you personally. Your umbrella policy is the last line of defense before your personal assets are at risk. The cost typically $300-$600 per year for $1-2 million in coverage is extraordinarily low relative to the protection provided. There is almost no Operator who cannot afford this and should not have it.

Disability insurance: is the most under purchased essential coverage among working people. The Social Security Administration estimates that more than one in four twenty-year-olds will become disabled before retirement age. Your ability to earn income, the engine that funds everything you're building is your single most valuable financial asset in your working years. Disability insurance replaces a portion of that income if you become unable to work. Get it. Group disability through an employer is a start; an individual policy (which stays with you regardless of employment) is better.

Life insurance: Term life insurance a death benefit payable for a specific period is the appropriate product for most Operators who have dependents relying on their income. Buy enough to replace your income for the years during which your family would need it, and select the term that matches your accumulation timeline (the period until your investment portfolio could sustain your family). Permanent life insurance (whole life, universal life) serves specific estate planning purposes for high-net-worth Operators and should be evaluated with your estate planning attorney rather than a life insurance salesperson.

Property and casualty insurance: for every investment property and business should be reviewed annually to ensure it reflects current values and current risks. Underinsurance a policy that covers less than the actual replacement cost of a property is a common and expensive mistake discovered only when a claim is made.

Estate Planning as an Operator Tool

Estate planning is not just something you do when you're old. It is an active Operator tool that serves multiple purposes throughout your financial life: protecting your assets during your life if you become incapacitated, specifying exactly how your assets pass to the people you choose at death, minimizing the tax cost of wealth transfer, and protecting your heirs from the legal and financial complexity of settling an estate without proper documentation.

The essential estate planning documents every Operator needs, regardless of age or wealth level:

A will specifies who inherits your assets and who manages your estate at death. Without a will, state law determines who inherits a distribution scheme that may not match your wishes and that may not reflect your relationships.

A revocable living trust avoids the public, court-supervised probate process and allows assets to pass directly to your heirs according to your instructions, without the delay and cost of probate. For most Operators with any meaningful assets, a living trust is worth the cost of establishment.

Durable power of attorney authorizes a person you designate to manage your financial affairs if you become incapacitated. Without this, a court process (guardianship or conservatorship) may be required expensive, public, and not of your choosing.

Healthcare directive and proxy specifies your medical wishes if you cannot communicate them and designates someone to make healthcare decisions on your behalf.

Beneficiary designations on retirement accounts, life insurance, and other assets that pass outside of your will should be reviewed and updated every time a major life event occurs. A beneficiary designation is the document that actually controls the distribution of these assets; an inconsistency between a will and a beneficiary designation is resolved in favor of the beneficiary designation.

THE PROTECTION PRINCIPLE

Asset protection planning that happens after a claim is made is almost always too late. Transfers made after a creditor claim exists may be challenged as fraudulent transfers and reversed. The time to build your legal and financial armor is before you need it; when you are growing, when the operation is healthy, and when the protective structures can be put in place without any appearance of evasion. Do not wait for the threat to arrive before building the defenses.

Chapter 16

The Generational Operation: Building Wealth That Outlasts You

"A society grows great when old men plant trees whose shade they know they shall never sit in."- **Greek Proverb**

Most financial planning thinks in years. The generational Operator thinks in decades. Plural. Not "how do I retire comfortably?" but "how do I build something that serves my children, my grandchildren, and potentially my great-grandchildren something that grows more powerful, not less, across generations?" This shift in time horizon changes everything: the investments you make, the structures you build, the values you transmit, and the conversations you have with your family about money, responsibility, and purpose.

Generational wealth is not an accident. It is not the automatic byproduct of building a lot of wealth. The research on inherited wealth is sobering: approximately 70% of wealthy families lose their wealth by the second generation, and approximately 90% lose it by the third. "Shirtsleeves to shirtsleeves in three generations" the folk wisdom about inherited wealth not lasting has substantial empirical support. The problem is almost never the wealth itself. The problem is the failure to transmit the knowledge, values, and governance structures that created and sustained the wealth.

The Difference between First-Generation Wealth and Generational Wealth

First-generation wealth is wealth built by someone who started from nothing or near-nothing is the product of specific skills, behaviors, and attitudes that developed in the crucible of scarcity. The first-generation wealth builder knows, in their bones, the value of money because they can remember not having it. They have the drive that comes from the gap between where they started and where they want to be. They have the discipline born of necessity.

Their children are born into a different world. They have never experienced scarcity. They don't carry the visceral memory that their parents carry. They inherited the wealth but not necessarily the attitudes, skills, and disciplines that created it. If those attitudes and skills are not deliberately transmitted through education, through structured financial responsibility, through genuine involvement in the family's financial operations the second generation often does not know how to steward what they've inherited. The third generation is often two or three more steps removed from the skills and values that mattered.

Building generational wealth means building the transmission mechanism alongside the wealth itself. The money is the easy part. The culture is the hard part.

Family Governance and Family Constitutions

The ultra-wealthy the families with wealth that has persisted across multiple generations typically have explicit governance structures: written documents and regular family meetings that define how the family's wealth is managed, how decisions are made, what values govern the family's approach to money, and how conflicts are resolved.

A family constitution also called a family charter or family governance document is a written statement of the family's values, purpose, and principles around wealth. It is not a legal document (though it may inform legal documents). It is a statement of identity: what the family stands for, what it is trying to accomplish with its wealth, and what principles will guide decisions across generations. The process of creating a family constitution which involves conversation, negotiation, and consensus-building among family members is often as valuable as the document itself, because it forces explicit discussion of questions that families usually avoid until a crisis makes avoidance impossible.

Regular family meetings financial education sessions for children, transparent discussion of the family's financial situation and decisions appropriate to their age, conversations about values and purpose build the financial literacy and family alignment that sustain generational wealth. The Rockefeller family, the Mars family, the Walton family - the families whose wealth has persisted and grown across generations - all have explicit family governance structures and cultures that prioritize financial education and shared values over simply distributing money.

Family Offices

The family office is the institutional structure through which the ultra-wealthy manage their financial affairs at scale. A single-family office (SFO) serves one family exclusively, typically requiring at least $100 million in investable assets to justify the cost of maintaining staff, systems, and infrastructure. A multi-family office (MFO) serves multiple wealthy families, pooling the cost and providing family-office-quality services at a lower entry threshold - typically $10-25 million.

The family office provides comprehensive services: investment management, tax planning and compliance, estate planning coordination, philanthropy management, family governance support, bill payment, insurance management, and concierge personal services for family members. For families with sufficient scale, it is a coherent and cost-effective alternative to managing multiple separate professional relationships. For most Operators, a family office is a future aspiration rather than a current reality - but understanding what it does and why helps you design your professional team at whatever scale you're currently operating.

Teaching the Next Generation to Operate, Not Just Inherit

The most important investment you make in your generational wealth is not financial, it is educational. Children who understand how money works, who have been given real financial responsibility at age-appropriate levels, who have been taught to think like Operators rather than consumers, are dramatically better positioned to steward and grow wealth than those for whom money was a silent background presence that simply appeared when needed.

Financial education of the next generation begins not with lessons but with modeling. Children watch how their parents talk about money, make decisions about spending, handle financial stress, and relate to their own wealth. The unconscious programming they receive from observation is more powerful than any explicit lesson. An Operator who has worked on their own financial psychology who has moved from a scarcity mindset to an abundance mindset, who manages money with intention rather than anxiety models the attitudes that will serve their children far better than any dollar amount they might inherit.

Structured financial responsibility - giving children real money to manage with real consequences, providing a genuine budget for categories they control, involving older children in age-appropriate discussions of family financial decisions - builds financial competence through practice rather than lecture. The child who has managed their own clothing budget since age thirteen and made mistakes with it has financial skills that no classroom can provide.

For wealth above a certain threshold, explicitly involving adult children in the family's financial operations - introducing them to the accountant and attorney, walking them through the investment portfolio, explaining the entity structures and estate planning is both an educational exercise and a practical succession planning step. The next generation should not encounter the family's financial complexity for the first time at a probate reading.

The Legacy Mindset: Thinking in Decades

The legacy mindset is the final shift in financial thinking that separates the Operator who builds for a lifetime from the Operator who builds for generations. It means making decisions not just on the basis of what serves you now, or even what serves your family now, but on the basis of what creates lasting value and positive impact over a time horizon that extends beyond your own life.

This shows up in investment decisions; the Operator who plants trees knowing they won't sit in their shade. It shows up in business decisions, building a company with a culture and governance that will outlast any individual leader. It shows up in charitable and philanthropic decisions; deploying capital toward causes and institutions that will compound in social value over decades. And it shows up in family decisions; the deliberate cultivation of the next generation's capacity to operate, not just to inherit.

The legacy mindset is not selfless, it is the longest possible definition of self-interest, one that includes not just your welfare but the welfare of those who will carry your name and values forward into the world after you're gone. It is the final expression of what it means to be an Operator: not just taking ownership of your own financial destiny, but extending that ownership across time and generations.

The Generational Operator's Three Obligations

Build wealth that can sustain the next generation. Build the knowledge and values that allow the next generation to steward and grow that wealth. Build the governance structures that prevent the wealth from becoming a source of family conflict rather than a source of family strength. All three are required. Any one of them alone is insufficient.

PART FIVE

The Philosophy of the Operator

Chapter 17

The Psychology of Power and Money

"Until you make the unconscious conscious, it will direct your life and you will call it fate." - **Carl Jung**

We have spent most of this book examining the external architecture of wealth: how the financial system works, what tools are available, how to build and protect an operation. Now it's time to examine the internal architecture because without addressing what happens between your ears, all the external knowledge in the world will underperform its potential. The most sophisticated tax strategy, the most perfectly structured portfolio, the most legally airtight entity structure all of it can be sabotaged by the one variable that is hardest to control: yourself.

This is not pop psychology. This is operational reality. The behavioral finance research of the past thirty years has documented, with remarkable consistency and rigor, that human beings make predictably irrational decisions around money and that these irrational decisions are not random errors. They are systematic, predictable patterns rooted in psychological mechanisms that evolved for a world that didn't have investment portfolios, tax codes, or leveraged financial products. Understanding these patterns is as important as understanding any financial concept covered in the previous chapters.

Why Most People Unconsciously Reject Wealth

Here is a proposition that sounds counterintuitive: most people who struggle financially are not doing so primarily because of external circumstances. They are doing so, in part, because of internal programs beliefs, attitudes, and psychological patterns around money that were installed early in life and that drive financial behavior in ways the conscious mind doesn't recognize.

These programs are ubiquitous and cross every demographic. The person who makes a good income but can never seem to save who finds that expenses somehow always expand to match earnings is not simply undisciplined. They may be unconsciously maintaining the income-to-wealth ratio that feels "normal" based on the environment they grew up in. The person who makes several hundred thousand dollars and still feels financially insecure is not just being neurotic they may be operating on a deeply installed belief that financial security is never truly achievable, a belief formed in childhood by watching parents who struggled. The person who wins a legal settlement or inherits money and loses it within a year or two is often unconsciously returning to what feels like their "natural" level a thermostat set point that pulls them back regardless of what the external world puts in their hands.

The research on lottery winners illustrates this dramatically. Multiple studies have found that lottery winners revert, over time, to approximately their pre-lottery level of financial wellbeing. Not always, and not inevitably but with striking consistency. The problem is not the money. The money is just a number. The problem is the internal context in which the money operates the beliefs, habits, and patterns that were built before the windfall arrived and that continue to govern financial behavior after it.

Common money beliefs that serve the financial system's interests, not yours:

- "Rich people are greedy/selfish/dishonest" any belief that associates wealth with negative character traits creates an unconscious aversion to becoming wealthy, because most people don't want to see themselves as greedy, selfish, or dishonest.

- "Money is the root of all evil" - a misquotation (the original is "the love of money is the root of all evil") that, taken literally, positions wealth as something morally suspect.
- "You have to work hard for money" - which subtly implies that money obtained without physical labor (investment returns, passive income) is somehow not earned or not legitimate.
- "I'm not good with money"- an identity statement that is often treated as fixed fact rather than as a skill gap that can be addressed.
- "We're not the kind of people who have a lot of money" perhaps the most insidious of all, because it frames wealth as something that belongs to other kinds of people, not people like you.

The Operator's work with these beliefs is not to pretend they don't exist. It is to bring them into conscious awareness to examine them, question their validity, and deliberately replace them with beliefs that serve your financial goals rather than undermine them. This is internal work that pairs with every external financial strategy. The two work together or they don't work at all.

The Scarcity-Abundance Spectrum

The scarcity mindset sees the world's resources as fixed and finite: every dollar you have is one less available to someone else, someone who succeeds near you is taking an opportunity that could have been yours, and financial security is always conditional, always at risk of being taken away. The scarcity mindset hoards not just money, but information, relationships, and opportunities out of a fundamental belief in insufficiency.

The abundance mindset sees the world's resources as expandable and renewable: value can be created, relationships can be mutually beneficial, someone else's success does not diminish yours, and the game of financial life has enough opportunity for many players. The abundance mindset is generous with information, connections, and credit because it understands that generosity in a world of creating value generates more value, not less.

The crucial point: neither mindset is simply a belief you choose, like picking a favorite color. Both are trained patterns, installed through experience, reinforced by behavior, and deeply resistant to simple "positive thinking" overwrites. Moving permanently toward abundance requires consistent behavioral evidence experiences of genuine generosity that are rewarded, risks taken that paid off, giving that came back multiplied. The behavior must precede the belief, because the belief won't change until the evidence does.

Practically: the Operator who gives generously with money, with knowledge, with connections, with time tends to live in a network of generosity, which creates a fundamentally richer experience of both wealth and community than the hoarder who accumulates in isolation. This is not just philosophy. It is the structural reality of how high-value networks work: they are built on reciprocal generosity, and the Operator who brings genuine value to their network receives genuine value in return over time.

Operator Identity vs. Consumer Identity

Identity is the most powerful driver of financial behavior. Not knowledge, not discipline, not willpower identity. What you believe you are determines what you do without conscious effort, because the behavior that is consistent with your identity feels natural and the behavior that is inconsistent with it feels forced. You don't have to remind yourself to brush your teeth in the morning it is consistent with your identity as a person who maintains their health.

You don't have to think about whether to steal something from a store your identity as an honest person makes the alternative feel unthinkable.

Consumer identity: the primary framework for evaluating financial decisions is "what can I afford to buy?" Income is money to be spent. Assets are a means to more consumption. Status comes from visible markers of spending. Financial decisions are made based on desire and immediate gratification, constrained by available credit.

Operator identity: the primary framework is "what does this do for my operation?" Income is capital to be allocated. Assets are the instruments through which wealth compounds. Status comes from what you've built, not what you consume. Financial decisions are made based on strategic fit, risk-adjusted return, and long-term impact on the operation.

The shift from consumer identity to Operator identity is not made by reading a book. It is made by repeated choices small and large that are consistent with Operator thinking, and the gradual accumulation of evidence that Operator thinking produces Operator outcomes. Each time you choose to invest instead of spend impulsively, each time you research before deciding, each time you think about your financial life in terms of building and protecting an operation, you strengthen the Operator identity and weaken the consumer identity.

Handling Success, Pressure, and the Social Cost of Outperforming

There is a specific psychological challenge that financial success creates that almost no financial book addresses honestly: the social cost of outperforming your environment. When your financial trajectory diverges from the people around you your family, your friends, your community you enter territory for which most people are not psychologically prepared.

Success creates distance. Not always, and not inevitably, but often enough that it deserves acknowledgment. The friends who were peers when you were all struggling may become uncomfortable with your success. Family members may react with jealousy, resentment, or requests that put you in positions of awkward obligation. The values and reference points that defined your world when you were less financially successful may feel increasingly irrelevant. Conversely, the world of high financial achievement — whatever it looks like in your specific domain — may carry its own cultural norms and pressures that feel alienating or exhausting.

The Operator who has not thought through their identity who is building wealth but not simultaneously building a clear sense of what they value, who they want to be, and what they are building the wealth *for* is particularly vulnerable to this pressure. They may unconsciously self-sabotage to remain comfortable in their original social environment. Or they may over-assimilate into a new economic environment and lose the grounding that made them effective. Neither outcome serves the operation.

The antidote is purpose. An Operator who is clear about why they are building for family, for freedom, for impact, for legacy has an anchor that holds across changes in financial status and social environment. The purpose doesn't change when the net worth number does. The purpose is the constant that gives the operation meaning beyond the accumulation of wealth for its own sake.

OPERATOR PSYCHOLOGY PRINCIPLE

Your internal architecture - your beliefs about money, your financial identity, your psychological relationship with wealth and risk is as important to your financial outcomes as your external strategy. The most sophisticated strategy in the world, operated by a person whose internal architecture is set to undermine it, will underperform. Do the internal work. It is not soft. It is the hardest and most important work in the operation.

Chapter 18

The Code of the Operator

"Power without wisdom is tyranny. Wealth without purpose is just weight." **The Operator's Creed**

We have arrived at the final chapter of the instructional portion of this book, and it is time to address the question that underlies everything we have discussed: not how to build wealth, but who you become in the process of building it, and what you do with it once you have it.

This is not a morality lecture. The Operator does not need to be lectured about ethics the Operator thinks carefully about ethics precisely because they understand the stakes involved in getting it wrong. Power including financial power without a clear ethical framework is not a stable state. It attracts attention, invites corruption, destroys relationships, and eventually collapses under the weight of its own contradictions. The history of financial operators who achieved extraordinary power and then lost it not to external market forces but to their own ethical failures is long enough to constitute its own cautionary canon.

The Code of the Operator is not an external constraint on ambition. It is the internal framework that makes ambition sustainable.

The Ethics of Operating in a System Designed to Exploit

We have spent much of this book examining the ways in which the financial system is designed to transfer value from less sophisticated participants to more sophisticated ones from retail investors to institutions, from debtors to creditors, from those who don't understand the rules to those who wrote them. Understanding this dynamic raises an ethical question that every Operator must answer honestly: what is the difference between using the system's rules intelligently and exploiting the people who don't know those rules?

This is a real distinction, not a rhetorical one. There are Operators whose success is genuinely built on superior knowledge, better strategy, and disciplined execution and there are "operators" whose success is built on the active exploitation of the uninformed, the desperate, or the vulnerable. The first category is legitimate and admirable. The second category is predatory and ultimately self-defeating, both morally and practically.

The practical reason exploitation fails: the financial system runs on trust and reputation. The Operator who builds a reputation for fair dealing, transparency, and genuine value creation has access to better relationships, better opportunities, and better capital than the one who generates short-term gains through exploitation. Over any meaningful time horizon, the ethical Operator outperforms the exploitative one not always in any individual transaction, but consistently across an operation and a career.

The moral reason exploitation fails: it corrupts the operator. The person who begins treating other people primarily as resources to be extracted as consumers to be manipulated, as counterparties to be taken advantage of, as obstacles or inputs rather than as human beings with legitimate interests loses something in themselves that is not easily recovered. The financial success that comes at the cost of integrity tends to feel hollow in ways that the person building honestly simply does not experience.

The Operator's ethical test is straightforward: would you be comfortable if every party to this transaction understood exactly what was happening and why? If yes, proceed. If not, if the transaction depends on the other party's ignorance, desperation, or incapacity to consent, do not proceed. This is not naivety. It is the operating principle of every sustainable Operator who has ever existed.

The Operator's Obligations

The financial success the Operator builds does not exist in a vacuum. It exists in the context of families, communities, and systems that made it possible the infrastructure, the legal frameworks, the educated workforce, the social trust and that deserve acknowledgment and reciprocation.

To family - The Operator's primary obligation is to the people who depend on them a partner, children, aging parents. Financial success that comes at the cost of these relationships is not success. The Operator who builds a financial empire at the expense of their marriage, their relationship with their children, or their own health is not an Operator they are a cautionary tale. The operation is built *for* family and community, not instead of them.

To community. Wealth creates capacity, and capacity creates obligation. The Operator who has financial resources has the ability to contribute to the community in ways that those without resources cannot. This is not about performative philanthropy or virtue signaling — it is about recognizing that communities and institutions are investments in the social infrastructure that makes everything else possible. The schools that educated the employees who work in your business, the hospitals that serve your family, the civic institutions that maintain the order within which your wealth is protected these are not separate from your financial operation. They are part of its foundation.

To legacy - The Operator's obligation to legacy is the obligation to leave the world or at least the corner of it they have operated in better than they found it. Not necessarily through grand gestures or famous philanthropy. Often through the quiet accumulation of honest dealings, genuine value creation, mentorship of the next generation of Operators, and the demonstration that it is possible to build significant financial success without compromising integrity.

How power is used and how it is lost

Financial power the kind this book has been building toward is real power. The ability to deploy capital, create jobs, fund projects, build communities, and provide security for multiple generations of your family is a form of power that few people in human history have held. Using it well requires the same clarity and intentionality that building it required.

Power is lost through several consistent mechanisms:

Hubris - The belief that past success guarantees future success. That your judgment, proven in the domain where you built your wealth, is equally reliable in other domains. That the rules which constrain others don't apply to you. The financial operators who have lost the most spectacular amounts of wealth from the historically famous to the regionally notorious have almost universally suffered from hubris in the period preceding their downfall. The Operator maintains the discipline of intellectual humility the recognition that being right about some things does not make you right about all things, and that the world is complex enough to humiliate the most accomplished operator if they stop learning and stop checking their assumptions.

Isolation - The tendency of successful people to surround themselves with people who agree with them, who validate their decisions, and who have financial interests in their continued approval. The Operator who has no one in their circle who will tell them hard truths who is universally surrounded by people who benefit from their success and are therefore constitutionally unlikely to challenge their thinking is flying without instruments. The correction mechanism is gone. And when the correction mechanism is gone, errors accumulate until they become catastrophic.

Drift from fundamentals - The discipline that builds the operation is sometimes abandoned once the operation is built. The Operator who built wealth through careful risk management and disciplined execution begins to take larger, less careful bets. The investor who built a portfolio through patient, fundamental analysis begins to chase momentum and novelty. The business builder who grew through relentless focus on customer value and operational excellence begins to lose interest in the details. Success creates the comfort that erodes the habits that created the success. The defense against drift is systematic — regular review of whether the operation is still being run on the principles that built it.

The Final Operator Principle: Domination Is Mastery of Self

We arrive at the final principle of this trilogy, the capstone of everything that has come before it.

World domination in the Operator's sense is not about defeating anyone. It is not about accumulating more than the next person, about winning a competition that exists only in the shallowest version of the financial game. It is not about status, about impressing anyone, or about the number on a net worth statement as an end in itself.

World domination is about mastery of self in the domain of financial life. It is the state of being in which your financial destiny is genuinely your own not dictated by external systems you don't understand, not derailed by psychological patterns you haven't examined, not constrained by ignorance of the tools available to you. It is the state of being in which you operate in the financial world with full situational awareness, strategic precision, ethical clarity, and genuine purpose.

This mastery is never complete. The world changes. Markets evolve. Tax laws change. Technologies disrupt. The Operator who achieved mastery at forty must continue earning it at sixty. The operation never reaches a state of permanent perfection, it is always under construction, always being adapted to the changing landscape of the world it exists within.

But the direction of the Operator's journey is always the same: deeper understanding, greater precision, more honest self-knowledge, clearer purpose. Each chapter of this trilogy has been a step in that direction. This final principle is not a destination, it is the understanding that the journey itself is the point. The Operator who embraces that understanding never truly stops growing. And an Operator who never stops growing is, by definition, an Operator who can never be stopped.

THE OPERATOR'S CODE - SUMMARIZED

Operate with complete integrity. Use the system's rules without exploiting other people. Build for your family, your community, and your legacy not just your balance sheet. Maintain the discipline that built the operation as the operation grows. Stay curious, stay humble, and never stop learning. Remember that every dollar of wealth is a tool for building the life and world you actually want, not an end in itself. And remember: domination is mastery of self. Everything else follows from that.

Conclusion

The Operation Never Ends

You have covered significant ground.

When Book 1 of this trilogy began, the goal was simple and enormous: change the way you think about money. Not just what you believe about personal finance tactics, but the foundational framework through which you interpret your financial life and your place in the economic world. The Operator's Blueprint was about installing the operating system the mindset, the identity, the core principles that make everything that follows possible.

Book 2, The Operator's Playbook, was the first layer of execution. We got tactical - Real estate, Business structure, Debt and credit and Income streams. The Operator's Playbook gave you the practical foundation for beginning to build a financial operation from wherever you were starting.

This book - the final volume of the Operator Edition Trilogy was the master level. We pulled back the curtain on the architecture of the global financial system: who built it, what it was built to do, and what it means for you as an

Operator navigating within it. We examined the tools at the top of the financial game: international markets, offshore structures, tax strategy, alternative assets, leverage, protection, and the generational operation. We studied the people who changed the game and those who failed spectacularly in attempting to. We built the philosophy that holds it all together.

Now it is your turn.

Not in some distant future when you have more money, more time, more confidence, more certainty about the right path. Now. Today. With what you have, where you are, with the knowledge you've acquired across these three books.

The journey of the Operator does not begin at some threshold of wealth or sophistication. It begins with the decision to take ownership - real ownership, not nominal ownership of your financial destiny. That decision is what separates the Operator from the participant. And you have already made it, or you would not have read this far.

Here is what "world domination" looks like in the first week after reading this book: you open the dashboard spreadsheet and fill in your net worth for the first time honestly, without omitting the uncomfortable numbers.

You schedule a meeting with a CPA who specializes in business and investment taxation. You review your entity structure and ask whether it is serving you or whether you are simply defaulting to however you happen to be structured. You look at your investment portfolio and ask honestly whether your allocation reflects a deliberate strategy or the accumulation of random decisions over time. You have a conversation with your partner or family about what you are building and why.

None of these things requires a large investment of money. They require a small investment of time and a significant investment of honesty. That is where the Operator's work always begins.

The financial system is not going to reform itself while you wait. The tax code is not going to simplify. Wall Street is not going to voluntarily stop using your order flow. Central banks are not going to publish their internal deliberations in plain English. The rules are what they are, and they will remain what they are until they change at which point an Operator adapts and continues operating, because that is what Operators do.

The challenge, offered in the spirit with which this entire trilogy was written:

Stop waiting for the perfect conditions. Stop waiting for the market to calm down, for the interest rates to be right, for the political environment to be more favorable, for the time when you have "enough" to start. The Operator who waits for perfect conditions is waiting for a condition that does not exist in financial markets and has never existed in human history. The conditions are always imperfect. The Operator operates anyway, because the alternative waiting is itself a decision, and its consequences are real.

You now know the rules. Not all of them no one knows all of them, and they're always changing anyway. But you know enough to play. You know enough to start building. You know enough to hire the right professionals and ask them the right questions. You know enough to see the system for what it is and to move through it with intelligence and intention rather than confusion and fear.

The operation never ends. That is not a burden it is the point. The Operator who remains engaged, who keeps learning, who keeps building and protecting and adapting and evolving, is the Operator who builds something that genuinely matters and genuinely lasts.
Go build it.

The operation continues.

Afterword

A Note on Continued Learning

A book, by its nature, is a fixed document in a moving world. By the time you read this, some of the specific details tax rates, regulatory requirements, market conditions, available technology platforms will have changed. That is not a failure of the book. It is the nature of financial knowledge, which lives at the intersection of permanent principles and constantly evolving specifics.

The permanent principles in this trilogy will not change: the power of compounding, the importance of tax efficiency, the danger of excessive leverage, the value of genuine diversification, the primacy of cash flow, the need for asset protection, the obligation to operate with integrity. These are structural truths about how wealth is built and preserved that have held across centuries, political systems, and technological revolutions. They will hold for your entire career.

The specifics will change. The tax code will be amended it always is. New financial instruments will emerge. Regulations will evolve. Technologies will disrupt old business models and create new ones. Geopolitical shifts will create new risks and new opportunities in global markets. The Operator who treats any specific piece of knowledge as permanent who stops updating their understanding because a book or a course told them everything they need to know is the Operator who gets left behind.

Stay curious. The financial and economic world rewards sustained intellectual engagement more generously than almost any other domain. Every hour you spend genuinely understanding how markets work, how businesses create value, how monetary systems function, and how wealth is preserved across generations is an hour that compounds through better decisions, better positioning, and better professional conversations for the rest of your life.

Build a reading practice. The bibliography at the end of this book is a starting point, not a complete curriculum. Beyond books, the primary sources company earnings calls and annual reports, Federal Reserve minutes and speeches, academic research in behavioral economics and financial theory, the regulatory guidance published by the IRS and SEC are more valuable than most secondary commentary. Going to primary sources is how Operators develop genuine understanding rather than summarized impressions.

Build a learning network. The people around you are the richest source of ongoing financial education available. Seek out mentors and peers who are operating at a level above your current position and learn from their experience. Participate in communities of serious Operators real estate investing groups, business owner networks, professional associations where genuine knowledge is exchanged. The right relationships will teach you more in a year than most courses can in five.

And above all: apply what you learn. Knowledge without application is trivia. The Operator who reads everything but does nothing is no closer to financial domination than the person who reads nothing. Every concept in this trilogy becomes more powerful the moment it is applied imperfectly, iteratively, in the real world with real stakes. The learning that matters is the learning that changes what you do.

The world is your classroom. The operation is your laboratory. Stay in school.

Glossary of Operator Terms

Accredited Investor - Under SEC rules, an individual with annual income exceeding $200,000 (or $300,000 joint) or net worth exceeding $1 million excluding primary residence. Accredited status unlocks access to certain private investments, including hedge funds and private placements, that are not available to the general public.

All-Weather Portfolio - An investment portfolio designed to perform adequately across all economic environments (rising growth, falling growth, rising inflation, falling inflation) by holding asset classes that each perform well in different conditions. Popularized by Ray Dalio and Bridgewater Associates.

Alternative Assets - Investment assets outside the traditional categories of publicly traded stocks and bonds. Includes real estate, private equity, private credit, hedge funds, commodities, infrastructure, farmland, and collectibles. Often provide diversification benefits due to lower correlation with public markets.

Asset Protection - Legal strategies and structures designed to shield assets from future creditor claims. Includes LLC structures, irrevocable trusts, exemptions under state and federal law, and in some cases offshore structures. Must be implemented proactively before any creditor claim exists.

Basis (Tax Basis) - Your cost in an asset for tax purposes. When you sell an asset, your taxable gain is the difference between your sale price and your basis. Strategies that increase basis (such as depreciation recapture adjustments) or reset basis (stepped-up basis at death) can significantly affect tax outcomes.

Bonus Depreciation - A tax provision allowing businesses to immediately deduct a large percentage (up to 100% in some years) of qualifying asset costs in the year of purchase rather than over the asset's standard depreciation life. Particularly powerful when combined with cost segregation in real estate.

Capital Gains - Profit from the sale of a capital asset (stock, real estate, business interest). Long-term capital gains (assets held more than one year) are taxed at preferential rates (0%, 15%, or 20% for most taxpayers) compared to ordinary income rates. Short-term capital gains (held one year or less) are taxed as ordinary income.

Carried Interest - The share of an investment fund's profits (typically 20%) that goes to the fund's general partners as compensation for managing the fund. Carried interest is taxed as capital gains rather than ordinary income, a treatment that has been debated politically for decades.

Cost Segregation - An engineering and accounting analysis that reclassifies components of real estate from the standard 27.5-year or 39-year depreciation schedules to shorter-life categories (5, 7, or 15 years), dramatically accelerating depreciation deductions in early years of ownership.

Credit Spread - The difference in yield between a corporate bond and a comparable Treasury security. Indicates the additional return investors require to hold credit risk. Widening spreads signal increasing market risk aversion; narrowing spreads signal increasing confidence.

Dark Pool - A private, off-exchange trading venue where large blocks of securities can be traded without public disclosure. Used primarily by institutional investors to minimize market impact of large orders. Contributes to price discovery fragmentation.

Donor-Advised Fund (DAF) - A philanthropic vehicle where a donor makes a tax-deductible contribution to a sponsoring organization, receives an immediate tax deduction, and then recommends grants to specific charities over time. Allows front-loading of charitable deductions in high-income years.

FBAR (Foreign Bank Account Report) - Annual FinCEN filing required of US persons with aggregate foreign financial account balances exceeding $10,000 at any point during the year. Failure to file carries severe civil and criminal penalties.

FATCA (Foreign Account Tax Compliance Act) - US law requiring foreign financial institutions to report accounts held by US persons to the IRS. Effectively ended most forms of offshore tax evasion through major financial institutions.

Fiduciary - A person legally required to act in another party's best interest. Investment advisors registered under the Investment Advisers Act are fiduciaries. Registered representatives (brokers) operating under FINRA are subject to a "suitability" standard, not a fiduciary standard an important distinction when selecting financial professionals.

Float - Money held by an insurance company between the time premiums are received and the time claims are paid. Warren Buffett famously used Berkshire's insurance float as essentially free leverage to fund investments. Float is an operating leverage concept with broad business applications.

Freedom Number - The annual passive/portfolio income level that equals or exceeds your desired lifestyle expenses, making employment optional. Calculated by multiplying desired annual spending by 25 (assuming a 4% sustainable withdrawal rate).

Fractional Reserve Banking - The banking system in which banks hold only a fraction of deposits as reserves and lend the remainder. Creates money multiplication — the economy's supply of money is far larger than the base currency issued by the central bank.

High Water Mark - In hedge fund fee structures, the previous peak value of the fund. Performance fees are only charged on gains above the high water mark, preventing the fund from charging performance fees on gains that merely recover previous losses.

Irrevocable Trust - A trust in which the grantor permanently gives up control of transferred assets. Because assets are removed from the grantor's estate and control, they may be protected from creditors and excluded from the taxable estate at death. Various types serve different estate planning purposes.

Leverage - The use of borrowed money to amplify investment returns (and losses). Leverage multiples both gains and losses by the leverage ratio. Understanding and controlling leverage is one of the most critical skills in the Operator's toolkit.

Liquidity Risk - The risk that an asset cannot be sold quickly at or near its estimated value. Highly illiquid assets may have attractive returns in normal conditions but can cause catastrophic losses when they must be sold under adverse conditions with no willing buyers.

Margin of Safety - Benjamin Graham's concept of buying securities at a significant discount to their intrinsic value, providing a buffer against errors in analysis and unfavorable developments. The wider the margin of safety, the more a situation can deteriorate before the investment becomes unprofitable.

Operator - An individual who takes complete, intentional ownership of their financial destiny. Not a passive participant in financial systems built by others, but an active architect of their own financial architecture — aware of the system, strategic in their approach, and building toward specific, defined goals.

Payment for Order Flow (PFOF) - The practice of brokerages receiving compensation from market makers for routing customer orders to them for execution. Creates a potential conflict between the broker's financial interest (routing to highest-paying market maker) and the customer's interest (best execution).

Qualified Business Income (QBI) - Under the Tax Cuts and Jobs Act of 2017, owners of pass-through businesses may deduct up to 20% of their qualified business income from federal taxable income. Subject to income thresholds, W-2 wage limitations, and industry restrictions. One of the most valuable provisions in the current tax code for business owners.

Quantitative Easing (QE) - A central bank policy of purchasing financial assets (typically government bonds and mortgage-backed securities) to inject money into the financial system and lower long-term interest rates. Used extensively by the Fed following the 2008 crisis and during the 2020 pandemic. QE tends to inflate asset prices, benefiting asset owners disproportionately relative to wage earners.

Revolving Door - The movement of individuals between positions as government regulators and positions in the private financial industry. Creates structural conflicts of interest in which regulators may be reluctant to take actions that would harm their future private sector prospects.

S-Corporation (S-Corp) - A corporation that elects pass-through tax treatment under Subchapter S of the Internal Revenue Code. Income and losses pass through to shareholders' personal tax returns. Salary paid to owner-employees is subject to payroll taxes; remaining distributions are not creating payroll tax savings relative to sole proprietorship or single-member LLC treatment.

Sovereign Wealth Fund (SWF) - A state-owned investment fund managing a country's national savings or commodity revenues. The world's largest SWFs Norway's Government Pension Fund Global, the Abu Dhabi Investment Authority, China's CIC manage trillions of dollars and are significant forces in global capital markets.

Stepped-Up Basis- When an asset is inherited, its tax basis is "stepped up" to its fair market value at the date of the decedent's death, eliminating the capital gains tax that would have been owed on any appreciation during the decedent's lifetime. One of the most significant wealth transfer benefits in the tax code.

Tax-Loss Harvesting - The practice of selling securities that have declined in value to realize a loss for tax purposes, then reinvesting in similar (but not identical, to avoid wash sale rules) securities to maintain portfolio exposure. Losses can offset capital gains and, up to $3,000 per year, ordinary income.

Yield Curve - A graphical representation of interest rates across different maturities of government bonds. A normal (upward-sloping) yield curve, where long-term rates exceed short-term rates, suggests economic expansion. An inverted yield curve, where short-term rates exceed long-term rates, has historically preceded recessions with strong consistency.

1031 Exchange - A provision of the Internal Revenue Code allowing real estate investors to defer capital gains taxes by rolling the proceeds from a sale into a like-kind replacement property within specified time limits (45 days to identify, 180 days to close). One of the most powerful legal tax deferral tools available to real estate investors.

Bibliography and Recommended Reading

Organized by Category -All Titles Verified Published Works

Investing: Foundations and Frameworks

Graham, Benjamin. The Intelligent Investor: The Definitive Book on Value Investing. Revised Edition. HarperCollins, 2006. The foundational text of value investing. Every serious Operator should read this, particularly Chapters 8 and 20 on market temperament and margin of safety.

Lynch, Peter, and John Rothchild. One Up on Wall Street: How to Use What You Already Know to Make Money in the Market. Simon & Schuster, 2000. A masterclass in how individual investors can find and evaluate investment opportunities using their own experience and observation, advantages institutional investors don't have.

Bogle, John C. The Little *Book of Common Sense Investing: The Only Way to Guarantee Your Fair Share of Stock Market Returns.* Updated and Revised. Wiley, 2017. The definitive case for low-cost index investing as the baseline strategy against which all other approaches must be measured.

Marks, Howard. *The Most Important Thing: Uncommon Sense for the Thoughtful Investor.* Columbia University Press, 2011. Marks, founder of Oaktree Capital, offers some of the most nuanced and honest thinking about risk, market cycles, and investment judgment available in published form.

Greenblatt, Joel. *The Little Book That Still Beats the Market.* Wiley, 2010. A highly readable introduction to value investing through the lens of return on capital and earnings yield the "magic formula" that has held up well across market environments.

Investing: Psychology and Behavior

Kahneman, Daniel. *Thinking, Fast and Slow.* Farrar, Straus and Giroux, 2011. The Nobel laureate's comprehensive account of the two systems of human thought — the intuitive and the deliberate — and how their interaction produces both brilliant judgments and systematic errors. Essential reading for understanding your own financial decision-making.

Thaler, Richard H., and Cass R. Sunstein. *Nudge: Improving Decisions About Health, Wealth, and Happiness.* Revised and Expanded Edition. Penguin Books, 2021. How the architecture of choice — the way options are presented — dramatically influences financial decisions, and how to design your own financial environment for better automatic outcomes.

Housel, Morgan. *The Psychology of Money: Timeless Lessons on Wealth, Greed, and Happiness.* Harriman House, 2020.

One of the best books written about the emotional and psychological dimensions of financial decision-making. Highly readable and immediately applicable.

Ariely, Dan. *Predictably Irrational: The Hidden Forces That Shape Our Decisions.* Revised and Expanded Edition. HarperCollins, 2009. Behavioral economics made accessible: how humans systematically deviate from rational financial decision-making and what to do about it.

Macro and Systems Thinking

Dalio, Ray. *Principles for Navigating Big Debt Crises.* Bridgewater Associates, 2018. Available free at Bridgewater's website. The most comprehensive and honest account of how debt cycles build and unwind, illustrated with detailed case studies of major financial crises. Dense but invaluable.

Dalio, Ray. *Principles: Life and Work.* Simon & Schuster, 2017. Dalio's explicit codification of the decision-making frameworks that built Bridgewater. Essential reading for any Operator interested in building systematic thinking into their operation.

Galbraith, John Kenneth. *The Great Crash 1929.* Mariner Books, 2009. Originally published in 1954, still the most readable account of the psychology, mechanics, and aftermath of the most catastrophic financial crisis in American history. The lessons are permanent.

Lewis, Michael. *The Big Short: Inside the Doomsday Machine.* W. W. Norton, 2010. The story of the 2008 financial crisis through the eyes of the few investors who saw it coming and positioned accordingly. A masterclass in contrarian analysis and institutional failure simultaneously.

Business, Strategy, and Wealth Building

Kiyosaki, Robert T. *Rich Dad Poor Dad: What the Rich Teach Their Kids About Money That the Poor and Middle Class Do Not.* Warner Books, 2000. Whatever its limitations as a precise tactical guide, this book changed the mental model of millions of readers around the distinction between assets and liabilities and the importance of financial education. Its foundational framework remains worth understanding.

Collins, Jim. *Good to Great: Why Some Companies Make the Leap and Others Don't.* HarperBusiness, 2001. The research-based account of what distinguishes companies that achieve sustained excellence from those that don't. The principles — disciplined people, disciplined thought, disciplined action — translate directly to the individual Operator's approach.

Thiel, Peter, and Blake Masters. *Zero to One: Notes on Startups, or How to Build the Future.* Crown Business, 2014. Thiel's contrarian framework for thinking about competitive advantage, monopoly, and the nature of genuine innovation. The Operator's business thinking benefits enormously from understanding how the most successful companies actually create and defend value.

Ferris, Timothy. *The 4-Hour Workweek: Escape 9–5, Live Anywhere, and Join the New Rich.* Expanded and Updated Edition. Harmony Books, 2009. Not a literal guide to working four hours per week, but a genuinely radical framework for thinking about productivity, automation, and the design of income systems that operate without constant personal intervention.

History and Power

Ferguson, Niall. *The Ascent of Money: A Financial History of the World.* Penguin Books, 2009. The most accessible and comprehensive narrative history of how financial institutions — banks, bond markets, stock markets, insurance — developed and shaped human civilization. Context that makes the architecture of the modern financial system legible.

Greene, Robert. *The 48 Laws of Power.* Viking Press, 1998. A study of how power is acquired, maintained, and lost across history. Not a prescriptive guide but an analytical framework for understanding the dynamics of power that operate in every domain including financial ones. Read with appropriate philosophical distance.

Acknowledgments

Books do not get written alone. They emerge from conversations, challenges, experiences, and the accumulated wisdom of everyone who has shaped the author's thinking along the way. This one is no different.

To the readers of *The Operator's Blueprint* and *The Operator's Playbook* the Operators who reached out with questions, who shared their results, who pushed back on ideas that needed pushing back on, and who asked the harder questions that made this final volume necessary: this book exists because of you. Your engagement made it clear that the conversation needed to continue, and that the deeper layer of the financial system deserved the honest examination this book attempts to provide. I am grateful for your trust and for your refusal to settle for surface-level answers.

To every mentor, teacher, and colleague some formally trained, some schooled entirely in the real world who shared knowledge generously and without the gatekeeping that keeps so many people from accessing the financial education they deserve: the generosity ripples forward. It is the foundation on which everything in this trilogy was built.

To the professionals- the accountants, attorneys, financial advisors, and specialists who reviewed portions of this work for accuracy and who continue to demonstrate that technical expertise and genuine client advocacy are not mutually exclusive: your contribution to the accuracy and integrity of this work is reflected on every page.

To everyone who picks up this book without a financial background, without a wealthy family, without institutional connections who comes to it with nothing but the determination to understand a system that was not designed with them in mind and to operate within it effectively and with integrity: you are the reason this was written. The knowledge in these pages belongs to you as much as to anyone. It always did. Now you have it.

The operation continues.